Hidden Dangers to Kids' Learning

Hidden Dangers to Kids' Learning

Parent Guide to Cope with Educational Roadblocks

Betsy Gunzelmann

ROWMAN & LITTLEFIELD EDUCATION

A division of

ROWMAN & LITTLEFIELD PUBLISHERS, INC.
Lanham • New York • Toronto • Plymouth, UK

PUBLISHED BY ROWMAN & LITTLEFIELD EDUCATION
A division of Rowman & Littlefield Publishers, Inc.
A wholly owned subsidiary of The Rowman & Littlefield Publishing Group, Inc.
4501 Forbes Boulevard, Suite 200, Lanham, Maryland 20706
http://www.rowmaneducation.com

Estover Road
Plymouth PL6 7PY
United Kingdom

Copyright © 2010 by Betsy Gunzelmann

All rights reserved. No part of this book may be reproduced in any form or by any electronic or mechanical means, including information storage and retrieval systems, without written permission from the publisher, except by a reviewer who may quote passages in a review.

British Library Cataloguing in Publication Information Available

Library of Congress Cataloging-in-Publication Data

Gunzelmann, Betsy, 1952-
  Hidden dangers to kids' learning : a parent guide to cope with educational roadblocks / Betsy Gunzelmann.
    p. cm.
  Includes bibliographical references.
  ISBN 978-1-60709-443-2 (cloth : alk. paper) — ISBN 978-1-60709-444-9 (pbk. : alk. paper) — ISBN 978-1-60709-445-6 (electronic)
  1. Education—Parent participation—United States. I. Title.
  LB1048.5.G86 2010
  371.19'2—dc22   2009031964

Printed in the United States of America

∞™ The paper used in this publication meets the minimum requirements of American National Standard for Information Sciences—Permanence of Paper for Printed Library Materials, ANSI/NISO Z39.48-1992.

As always this book is dedicated to my mother, Mary Gunzelmann, my rock when times got tough, and my son, Matt Gunzelmann, who gives depth and purpose for researching, writing, and for being.

The journey of life is full of opportunities and pitfalls. Be true to those who care most and be true to self, then you'll be making the right choices.

Contents

Dedication	v
Acknowledgments	ix
Reader's Note	xi
Introduction	xv

Part I: Smart Kids Failed By Our Schools		**1**
Chapter One	New Reasons to Believe in Your Child and New Possibilities for Academic Success	3
Chapter Two	Is This Your Child? Understanding Hidden Dangers That Sabotage Your Child's Learning	7
Part II: Are Hidden Problems in Our Schools Negatively Affecting Your Child's Learning?		**13**
Chapter Three	Researched-Based Foundation to Understand the Needs of Children in School	15
Chapter Four	Misguided Assumptions, Attitudes, and Procedures that Negatively Impact Smart Kids	25
Chapter Five	Hidden Dangers in Testing that Impact Your Child	37
Chapter Six	Hidden Dangers with Labeling that Can Harm Your Child	47

Chapter Seven	Gender Problems that Affect Your Child's Learning	55
Chapter Eight	Paradoxical Safety Problems that Affect Student Learning	63
Chapter Nine	Building Problems that Negatively Impact Your Child's Learning	73

Part III: What Can We Do As Parents for the Short term and for Long-Term Improvement? — **81**

Chapter Ten	System Overhaul: Developing a Healthy School	83
Chapter Eleven	Transcending Dangers: Improvement for All Students	95
Chapter Twelve	Options/Alternatives for Parents of Kids Struggling in School	99
Appendix	Annotated Resources and Contact Information	109
References		113
About the Author		123

Acknowledgments

I am indebted to so many that helped to make *Hidden Dangers to Kids' Learning: Parent Guide to Cope with Educational Roadblocks* a reality. The children and parents who have shared their stories over the years form the core of my understanding of the hidden dangers in our schools; to all of you I am sincerely thankful. To my teachers and mentors who have guided me to a search for deeper knowledge, never being satisfied with surface learning . . . I thank all of you.

To my professional colleagues who have respected my need to research and to write. Specifically, Dr. Karen Erickson, Dean of Liberal Arts at Southern New Hampshire University, has been most supportive and encouraging; and to Jill Judd for her assistance with proofing and helping with the needed formatting changes. My colleagues have also been my sounding board allowing me to share my insights and ideas. You are my reality check to see if you too have seen and/or experienced such problems in our schools. Specifically, Drs. Diane Connell and Michael Noonan deserve a grand round of applause. I am most beholden to you both.

To my students and student researchers at Southern New Hampshire University who have assisted me with interviewing and synthesizing the information gathered . . . I am grateful. Specifically, Nicole Sanborn, now a graduate student, worked tirelessly on gathering information.

To the people at Rowman & Littlefield; specifically Tom Koerner, Vice President of Rowman & Littlefield Education, I am most indebted to your support and belief in my work. Maera Stratton and Melissa McNitt, I thank you for your tireless efforts and expertise in technical editing and production. Without your help this work could not have been brought to print.

To my friends who have supported my need for time to write and unfalteringly provided support and encouragement. Particularly, Tom and Rose Clarie, Kathy and John Gallagher, Susan and Bryan Simmonds and MaryPat King. Your friendships are gifts and we can all celebrate in our accomplishments.

And to my family, I thank you, appreciate you and love you more than you can know. You have provided all the right conditions at home with your unwavering love.

Reader's Note

The stories of the children in *Hidden Dangers to Kids' Learning: Parent Guide to Cope with Educational Roadblocks* are composites from listening and observing children who have experienced school problems over the years. Any resemblance noticed between these cases and children you may know is unintentional. The reader should understand that these stories are quite widespread in our schools and indeed shows us that hidden dangers affect many children.

Portions of this book have appeared in other publications and are reprinted with permission:

- "New possibilities for a new era: Research-based education for equity and excellence," Educational Horizons 88(1):21–27.
- *"Hidden dangers: Subtle signs of failing schools,"* 2008. Rowman & Littlefield form the basis of this parent guide and are included throughout the book.
- "Hidden problems in failing schools." *Educational Horizons:* 86(2): 85–97.
- "Toxic testing: It's time to reflect upon our current testing practices." *Educational Horizons,* 83(3), 212–220, forms the starting point for chapter 5 and parts throughout the book.
- "The new gender gap: Social, psychological, and educational perspectives." *Educational Horizons,* 84(2), 94–101, parts now incorporated in chapter 7 and throughout the book.
- "Hidden Dangers within our schools: What are these safety problems and how can we fix them?" *Educational Horizons,* 83(1), 66–76, forms the basis for chapter 8 and parts of it are incorporated throughout the book.

Introduction

Are you concerned about your child's education? Do you know that your child has more potential than is demonstrated in school? Is your child turned off by school? Is his/her childhood curiosity, love for learning being extinguished? If so, this book is for you! *Hidden Dangers to Kids' Learning: Parent Guide to Coping with Educational Roadblocks* is a valuable resource to help parents understand and navigate the perils and pitfalls of our educational system.

To the parents of kids affected by hidden dangers in our schools, I originally wrote *"Hidden Dangers: Subtle Signs of Failing Schools"* for teachers, administrators, professors of teacher education programs and for our country's leaders and policy makers. As time passed and I've had time for more reflection and research, I now realize that we not only need a top-down reorganization of our educational programs (which takes time), we need to begin with a bottom-up approach. We don't have time to waste—we are losing some of our country's greatest potential. We are losing many of our brightest students who are failing (or only doing mediocre work) in our schools. These children have such potential, but are being turned off—not shown how to think, how to learn, how to reach their unique potential.

This is why I have decided to rework parts of *"Hidden Dangers: Subtle Signs of Failing Schools"* into a guide for the parents of these struggling children. For parents are our children's best advocates. They, along with their children, can make changes now. Much is within their control as we shall see. *Hidden Dangers to Kids' Learning: Parent Guide to Cope with Educational Roadblocks* is a resource with which they can come to understand that the problems may lie not with their child, but with the system . . . and it is designed to empower them to find the solutions to help their children thrive academically . . . to become all they were meant to be.

I suppose it is typical for parents to believe the experts in the schools, to believe in the testing scores, to believe in the diagnoses that may be given your child, blaming him for his failure to learn. But don't ever lose sight of the fact that you are the expert on your child; you know your child almost better than anyone else (with the exception of the child him/herself). Test scores are fallible; misdiagnoses are all too common, yet are given as an explanation for why the school intervention did not work. It is different with strep throat where one either has it or doesn't and can be given an antibiotic to clear the infection. Learning diagnoses are not this straightforward . . . and finding the best approach to learning can be a challenge.

So, why are our schools failing these children? Yes, it is fair to say, even more correct to say the schools are failing these children . . . not that the children are failing. However, just as we must be careful not to blame our children for their school difficulties (for blame in most cases is not justified and only further distances children from wanting to succeed), we must also understand that placing blame on our teachers is unwarranted as well. Most of our teachers are trying to do good work, but find themselves under prepared and trying to fix problems by using a band-aid approach when a tourniquet is needed!

In the chapters ahead you will learn of many of the subtle problems sabotaging your child's education. You will also learn what can be done to help find solutions for your child and all children. *Hidden Dangers to Kids' Learning: Parent Guide to Cope with Educational Roadblocks* was written for you! You may have additional insights, comments, or questions. I welcome your ideas. Please e-mail me at: b.gunzelmann@snhu.edu.

Part I

Smart Kids Failed by Our Schools

Chapter 1

New Reasons to Believe in Your Child and New Possibilities for Academic Success

Hidden Dangers to Kids' Learning: Parent Guide to Cope with Educational Roadblocks marks a new beginning; a way for parents to understand and help their academically struggling child. Parents and their children can be empowered to recognize the perils and pitfalls of our current educational crisis and take charge of their education before it is too late. We have new reasons to believe in our children and new possibilities to expect and help our children to be able to cope in our global community.

Since the writing of *Hidden Dangers: Subtle Signs of Failing Schools* two years ago, we have undergone some remarkable changes within our country which bring the possibility for significant educational changes for our children. Our new administration in Washington is wasting no time addressing these concerns. However, fixing our schools is a complex problem and we need solutions which allow for choice and flexibility for all students ... and we need these alternatives now. (Gunzelmann, 2009)

If your child is one of the many smart kids currently underachieving in American schools, I want you first of all to understand that you are not alone! There are thousands of parents and children facing the same problems. Secondly, you must also understand the complexity of the issues so that you do not change your viewpoint about your child, so that you continue to believe in your child's abilities and maintain high expectations. Please keep believing in your child and his/her abilities. He/she needs your support now more than ever! Thirdly, once you have some inside knowledge about the problems in our schools, which involve often very subtle issues that prevent student achievement, you will be in a unique position, as an expert on your child, to advocate for him/her to gain access to the right approaches and programs that will allow him/her to succeed!

The reason I originally wrote *Hidden Dangers: Subtle Signs of Failing Schools* was so educators might have a glimpse into the possible reasons for student failure and underachievement and thus make the needed changes. But as we know, historically educational institutions are among the slowest to make significant changes. We do not have the time to lose even one student to the current epidemic of mediocrity and educational decline. This epidemic is the result of misunderstood research, faulty assumptions and policies, and other subtle causes of school failure that are currently impacting our students and the future of our country.

Many parents are very worried about their children, knowing that their children are smart (in many cases very smart), yet performing well below expectations. So, what are the new possibilities and reasons to believe? We are aware that fixing our schools is a multifaceted problem. We now have cutting edge research from related interdisciplinary fields of neuroscience, psychology, pediatrics and education. The gain made in brain-based studies and knowledge acquired from global education studies will strongly influence the delivery approaches within the classroom and with teacher education programs in the future. Additionally, we are finally beginning to bridge the gap between research and practice in the area of education. Such research-based initiatives offer hope for real change (Gunzelmann, 2009).

Our new administration in Washington is well aware that many international students are soaring ahead of our students educationally. The United States used to be the world leader in education. Now, according to the most recent PISA Assessment (Program in International Student Assessment), the United States students ranked 35th in math and 31st in science out of the top 40 countries participating (http://www.internationaled.org/PISA.html, Darling= Hammond, 2008). These alarming results show even further decline since the previous results in 2003. Research on global education is beginning to shed light on the reasons for the significant academic gains made in these thriving countries. It appears that all have curriculum, teaching approaches and teacher preparation programs that are based upon research, are equally available to all children and in-school and out-of-school resources are strongly supported by government funds (Gunzelmann, 2009). We need to do the same for our children.

President Barak Obama has a strong research-based educational policy built upon reform and accountability. His plan illustrates his reflective, flexible approach ... and it is sound. He is addressing the often overlooked needs of early childhood which will support infants and young children along with their parents to help assure children are educationally ready. The new plan will reform and support education for all children, allowing for individualizing educational interventions and making successful alternatives more readily available. Teacher preparation programs will be overhauled and our excellent teachers will finally gain the support and recognition they deserve (www.whitehouse.gov/agenda/education, 2009). His plan will support and reform the educational needs of our children "from the cradle up through a career" as well (Obama, 2009, CNNPolitics.com). But these changes will not come overnight.

Another hopeful sign of this new educational initiative is that it does not place blame. "We have let our grades slip, our schools crumble, our teacher quality fall short and other nations outpace us ... the time for finger pointing is over; the time for holding ourselves accountable is here" (Obama, 2009, CNNPolitics.com). Remember we should not be placing blame either since it is really just passing the buck from one source to another, increasing defensive behavior, anger and hurt, all of which prevent constructive change from occurring. We need to take responsibility now to help our children thrive academically, but also to understand what was mistaken and ineffective so that we do not keep repeating the same blunders.

So, what can you as parents do to help your child beginning right now ... particularly if your child is one of those who might still fall through the cracks of a school that just does not "fit" your child? This is what you will learn about in the following pages of *"Is This Your Child? Smart Kids Failed By Our Schools: A Guide for Parents."* Let's begin by reading the following poem as a way to reawaken your belief in your child; for you must believe in your child if you are going to help him/her succeed.

WHAT CHILDREN NEED

Listen to your children;
For they need to tell you of the troubles that they encounter every day.
Hear the unspoken words underneath their anger and frustration.
Watch your children;
For they need to show you what it's like to be misunderstood.
See the hurt in their anxious and withdrawn behavior.
Appreciate your children;
For they need to succeed, but doubt themselves.
Know that they are capable if guided with care and patience.
Remember what it was like when you were young;
For the children need to learn from our experiences.
Understand too, that it is different now; the pressures and problems are more complex.
Share your mistakes and struggles with your children,

So they need not feel so alone.
Offer them support and understanding.
Model responsible behavior for your children;
Because they need to learn to be conscientious too.
Support their hard work and persistence.
Value the uniqueness of your children;
Because they need to learn to understand themselves and others.
Appreciate the diversity of all; while knowing we are really more alike than different.
Be there for your children;
For they need you now more than ever.
Take time to let them know they are respected and understood.
Believe in your children;
Because they need to believe in themselves and have hope for the future.
Instill a sense of confidence, love and community so they will do the same for others.

(Gunzelmann, 2007)

We do have new reasons to believe and new possibilities for our children's futures. So, let's get on with our understanding of the reason so many of our children have been failed by our schools; for to help them succeed, we must learn from these lessons. We also must understand that:

There are no failures, only lessons to be learned.
— Oprah Winfrey
http://www.brightquotes.com/fai_fr.html, accessed March 13, 2009

Chapter 2

Is This Your Child? Understanding Hidden Dangers That Sabotage Your Child's Learning

"If you are happy with the way things are in the schools, and your children are happy and fulfilled, fine. I'm glad you are happy, and the schools are doing what you want them to for you. But there are lots of people out there who are very unhappy...."

—John Holt

KEVIN*

Kevin is a 12 year old boy from a two-parent, professional family. He enjoys several close friendships with his classmates at school and within his neighborhood. His interests include computer games, cars, and sports. Homework is often a struggle, but once he gets started he seems to complete the rather meaningless assignments without too much effort or thought.

Kevin sounds like a typical preadolescent child, yet he is a child who scores well below average academically. He does not have any learning disability, emotional or behavioral problems. To many parents and teachers this scenario may sounds quite familiar; it actually occurs rather frequently in schools. However, because it is a common phenomenon we should not assume it is not a serious problem. It is a grave crisis when a child is not learning and becomes frustrated, angry, anxious or depressed . . . and the rest of the child's life is affected! And it's happening to more and more of our children!

---

*Note: The cases in the book are composite sketches of children I have known and interviewed over the years. They are exemplary kids to portray the hidden issues involved and I firmly believe they represent only the tip of the iceberg with regards to the issues involved in toxic schools.

So, what is going on? Why isn't Kevin learning up to expectations? After all, he doesn't have any serious behavioral problems; on intelligence tests he scores well above average, he has friends and a supportive, caring family. At first his parents blame Kevin . . . since it is he who is not achieving up to expectation. But after some reflection they realize that it may not be Kevin's fault. Kevin seems to enjoy learning almost any subject that he has not been taught in school. He seems to read and write well, although often does not complete assignments for school. He is very well-behaved both at home and at school, and shows no signs of a passive-aggressive attitude, or desire to sabotage his learning. So, both his parents and his teachers are a bit puzzled by Kevin's lack of academic achievement.

His teachers, although usually well-intentioned, also seem to react in a similar manner. They do not ask what might be wrong with their approach to teaching, their classroom, the school, or the system. Rather, they immediately start looking for what is wrong with Kevin. The school psychologist may be called in to test the child. Although these tests are geared toward finding both strengths and weaknesses, it seems that the weaknesses are usually more the focus for schools and unfortunately many adults put more faith in the results of testing than is warranted. Tests do not always show us accurate results for a variety of reasons that we will consider in a later chapter. However, with all the limitations of testing, which there are many, comes a label or a diagnosis . . . oftentimes this too is inaccurate. Once labeled, the child becomes the diagnosis. Teacher expectations change; and even more sadly, parental expectations change and the child begins to doubt him/herself.

Years of being misunderstood and poorly educated can easily lead to a variety of secondary psychological and learning difficulties including the following: anxiety, depression, frustration, boredom, bullying, violence, problems with self-esteem, poor academic achievement and dropping out of school, to name just a few of the difficulties encountered by misunderstood children attending toxic schools. Clearly, we can see from the case of Kevin that he is an underserved child in a school setting that does not fit his needs . . . and Kevin is definitely not alone!

Kevin's parents believe their child has had several good teachers, but they (the teachers) were limited in what they could accomplish because of the dysfunctional climate at each school. Many critics would say that these students and parents are only seeing the negative issues, that they don't understand the complexities of the schools, and that they are not objective because the problems involve their children. Indeed, this is a good point, but is not always an accurate position.

Fortunately for Kevin, his parents took his concerns seriously, yet did not overreact by looking for pathology where none existed. They simply changed his school setting, finding a much better fit for their child.

Kevin blossomed in his new educational setting. Additionally, he was able to keep his old friends, while making several new ones. He also became confident with his work; indeed, he began to show the gifted side that his parents always knew was there, but which previous teachers were not able to see. Kevin became motivated and was excited about learning; in fact learning became his hobby . . . his life force.

There were no longer time boundaries to the school day . . . learning continued with excitement for Kevin throughout all the waking hours of his day, late into the night and even on weekends. He was a kid who went from getting poor (and in some cases failing) grades, to excelling with his studies. Kevin demonstrated an insatiable thirst for knowledge, for learning, for writing, and for being involved with helping others through experiential learning work. His parents no longer had to remind him to buckle down and start his homework. Instead their comments changed to "Don't you think you've done enough? Come and watch a little TV with us," and "It's really time to turn off that computer and the lights!"

Learning/life became an exciting adventure. Kevin is excited about his future, optimistic, and feeling safe and secure in his environment and with himself. (Although in Kevin's case he had to change schools to find an environment that was healthy for him, ideally it is best to address the problems within the school's climate so that all children can thrive. Keep in mind that positive changes in school climate will benefit all students, not just students who are showing symptoms.)

Why is it that so many children do not look forward to attending school once they are out of first grade? Why is learning a tedious process and not one full of joy for most children? I believe we are having a crisis in our schools, unprecedented from other times in history. We are seeing more violence than ever before, more diagnoses of learning difficulties, more ADHD and other behavioral and emotional problems. We have more concerns with students not attaining basic skills in reading, writing, and mathematics, or skills needed for success in our technologically oriented society. Although we live in the richest nation on earth, the academic achievement of our children is lagging well behind youth from many other countries around the world.

This crisis is well known to informed government officials, educators and parents alike. Back in 1983 the National Commission on Excellence in Education made the following statement:

> The educational foundations of our society are presently being eroded by a rising tide of mediocrity that threatens our very future as a nation and as a people . . . If an unfriendly foreign power had attempted to impose on America the mediocre educational performance that exists today, we might well have viewed it as an act of war. As it stands, we have allowed this to happen to ourselves." (April, 1983)

There have been numerous educational reform attempts over the years to rectify the problems, including President Clinton's *Goals 2000.* The most recent nationwide effort involves President Obama's *Education for the 21st Century* and it holds much promise for the future of our children and ultimately for our country. However, it will take time for the changes to be established and more time to see how well the new initiative(s) are working. There is much to research, remedy and revise since the *No Child Left Behind Act* signed by President G.W. Bush on January 8, 2002. Like previous educational reform acts, it was intended to improve schools, this time by focusing more on accountability, measurement of student progress, utilizing proven educational methods, and allowing for more freedom for states and communities and choices for parents. This mandate may have looked good upon first glance, but it actually contributed to our previous problematic conditions and exacerbated many of the difficulties experienced by children in our schools.

Although test results are showing some improvement for many students, these results come at a high cost of decreased depth to learning and lowered motivation. NCLB decreased the time teachers had to work to help students develop critical and analytical thinking skills. Teachers needed to teach to the test, utilizing a testing format that many of our deepest and most creative students often do quite poorly on! No Child Left Behind left many students behind and it did not aid the educational pursuit for excellence in our schools as intended!

Educational policies should not come down to a power struggle between our political parties. Government policies have all attempted to improve our schools, but when we look back over the years it appears that each incoming administration tends to undo the progress made by previous administrations. It is clearly time that we stop getting caught up in the politics of education and start looking at what is really happening in our schools. We need to hear from the experts who work most closely with children: the school administrators, school psychologists, counselors, teachers, parents and the children themselves. These are the true educational experts that know the inner workings of their schools; these are the people who can make the difference if given the opportunity to challenge current ideas, policies and practices. These educational experts coupled with cutting edge research from neuro science, psychology, and pediatrics should be our guide for new educational policy (Gunzelmann, 2009).

After many years working and volunteering in both public and private school settings, interviewing clients in private practice, and teaching and researching at both the graduate and undergraduate levels, I am concerned with what I am hearing from school administrators, clinicians, teachers, children, and their parents. Many "normal, typical" children are experiencing difficulties coping and learning in their traditional school setting. These children should be our "red flags" or the canaries in the coal mine, alerting us to the fact that our schools are in serious trouble.

We need to take a clear-headed look at our schools and the problems our youth are experiencing. We need to stop placing the blame outside of the schools and looking at the attitudes, the beliefs, policies and practices that guide our schools and the impact upon each school's unique environment. By understanding the whole picture and the impact on each school's climate, we can make all schools places where children learn and like to be, and where professionals can take pride in doing their best work.

What makes a superior school environment, where children are safe, learn the basics, and are challenged to their fullest potential? What possibly can be so unique and work so successfully at some schools that students can hardly wait to get there, experience a sense of community and shared responsibility, and where learning is both broad and deep in scope? Certainly, large public schools must address enormous problems, and most have limited financial resources to do so. However, it is possible for healthy conditions to occur in all schools and although money can be helpful, it does not assure an optimal learning environment.

So, how do we go about making the changes in our schools so that all children experience a sense of joy with learning? First, we must understand that what makes a school toxic to learning is a complex phenomenon to get your arms around. It's like trying to grasp a constantly moving and changing ball of wiggling slimy worms. One of the keys lies in understanding the school's climate. School climate is not a new concept. It has been defined in a number of ways over the years. Originally, climate and environmental studies fell within the parameters of Industrial/Organizational Psychology. However, over the last several decades schools have become increasingly concerned with climate issues as more and more difficulties needed to be handled in the school setting.

We all know from our own experiences that each school has a unique "feel" or "personality" ... some seem comfortable, safe and thriving ... while others evoke feelings of anxiety. So, what exactly do we mean when we talk of school climate? Peterson and Skiba (2001) view school climate as a reflection of positive and negative feelings regarding the school environments that directly and indirectly affect a variety of learning outcomes. I choose to look even more broadly and define school climate as a unique combination of intellectual, behavioral, social, political, ethical, and physical characteristics of a setting which is highly influenced by the society in which this school is located. I also use the term "toxic" to refer to hidden dangers which interfere with learning and the general mission of the school. Likewise, the term "healthy" refers to elements which enhance learning and the general mission of the school.

The climate of a school is easy enough to define, but it is a difficult and elusive phenomenon to identify. So let's take a closer look at children who were exposed to subtle toxic school conditions: typical students who were not thriving!

In the next chapters we will begin to discover why some schools have hidden dangers that interfere with optimal learning. Schools and classrooms vary greatly. One school may be producing students that are excelling, excited learners. Others, even in the same school district, having the same policies, are experiencing student failure and increasing dropout rates. Furthermore, some schools may contain both toxic and healthy conditions within the same building. The answers become clearer when we establish a solid foundation to understand children's basic needs, learning styles, and the need to foster/teach resilience, optimism and flexibility.

Most Americans have no idea how bad things really are. We are in a state of emergency. I'm blown away that this isn't what is on every parent's mind when it comes to elections . . . that people are not in the streets fighting for their kids.

—Oprah Winfrey, regarding her special report,
"American Schools in Crisis"

Part II

Are Hidden Problems in Our Schools Negatively Affecting Your Child's Learning?

Chapter 3

A Research Based Foundation to Understand the Needs of Children in School

"Modern cynics and skeptics... see no harm in paying those to whom they entrust the minds of their children a smaller wage than is paid to those to whom they entrust the care of their plumbing."

— John F. Kennedy

In many ways it seems we have not progressed too far from these enlightened words of the 1960's. Teachers are still underpaid and although students have made progress in some areas, they have lost ground in others. So let's take a closer look at the underlying issues. I firmly believe it is essential to obtain all sides of the story to fully comprehend a problem, but there is no need to reinvent the wheel in order to understand the troubles in our schools today.

If we have a solid understanding of the research and work from some of the best researchers and practitioners from the interdisciplinary fields of psychology, education, and child health, as well as insight into the mistakes of previous educational reform including *No Child Left Behind*, we will have a firm foundation upon which we can begin to understand the hidden dangers within our schools. Therefore, before I share my own work, I want to apply the insights and research from several groundbreaking specialists in the fields of medicine, psychology and education.

Boston Children's Hospital pediatrician T. Berry Brazelton and child psychiatrist Stanley Greenspan have contributed greatly by identifying the irreducible needs of children. We need to thoroughly understand these needs and make sure each is met in our schools. According to Brazelton and Greenspan (2000) there are seven irreducible needs that every child must have in order to grow, learn, and flourish. Although their work was developed to express children's necessities in all aspects of their lives, clearly school occupies a large part of most children's time and many of these basic needs are not being met in our schools!

These irreducible needs are as follows:

1. Every child needs ongoing, nurturing relationships.
2. Children need physical protection, safety, and regulation.
3. Children need experiences tailored to individual differences.
4. Children need developmentally appropriate experiences.
5. Children need boundaries, structure, and high, but reasonable expectations.
6. Children need stable, supportive communities and cultural continuity.
7. Children need protection for the future, while maintaining and supporting growth. (Brazelton & Greenspan, 2000)

At first glance these needs appear obvious, yet so many of them are not met for our children in our schools! These basic, irreducible needs should be the foundation upon which we build our schools. However, I want to explain how these needs are being undermined. Let's begin with the first one. Certainly children need primary caregivers who are there for them for the long haul. However, they also need committed teachers who see their students through the school year and beyond, and who are able to develop healthy, motivating relationships with them. They also need committed administrators who are available to assist with parent, student, and community concerns.

Unquestionably there are school personnel who are thoroughly committed to our children and they do make a difference, but too many are there just to receive their paycheck and many must hurry off to second jobs to make ends meet at home. Working with our children in the schools must be seen as one of the most important jobs in the world, second only to that of the parents.

Naturally kids need physical protection, safety and regulation, but are some of the practices in our schools undermining this need? I think the answer is a resounding yes! Since September 11th, 2001 school policies have changed dramatically in an attempt to provide a safe environment. However, school lock downs, metal detectors, and other such policies are in fact making many children feel as if they are constantly in danger. Children also need safe, non-toxic buildings for health and learning. Unfortunately, many of our nation's schools are sub par on this issue due to the high cost of needed updating and repairs for problems involving asbestos, toxic molds and other hazards.

Physical protection, safety and regulation also means that children need to be effectively protected from teasing, taunting, and disruptive behavior. Related to this problem, teachers should not be expected to, nor are they capable of, helping all children. Regular classroom teachers have not been trained to handle children with severe behavioral and emotional disturbances, and ultimately all children are put in a compromised situation. Children cannot learn successfully in settings where their basic need for protection is not met!

Applying the third need for experiences tailored to individual differences to our schools, we are aware that children need to feel respected for their individual areas of strength and weaknesses and have proper assistance to develop all areas to the fullest. Unfortunately, in many schools, I believe we are only giving lip service to this basic need. All children learn differently; understanding and flexibility are required. For example many children find it difficult to sit still during the early years. Blaming and misdiagnosing them with ADHD is harmful. Such constant misunderstanding and awkwardness of fit with one's academic environment may lead to a self-defeating downward spiral resulting in lowered academic performance for both boys and girls.

Some children indeed have ADHD and are in need of assistance, but far too many children are diagnosed with this disorder than is statistically likely. Many of our schools really believe that individual differences are indeed well addressed, but I believe that most schools do a very poor job valuing the uniqueness of each individual and in many cases are actually harming the child's capacity to learn.

The fourth basic need is another one schools believe is well addressed, but I beg to differ. All we need do is look at a typical first grade classroom where all children are expected to learn the same material at the same time. Since children develop at different ages all are not ready to read or write or sit still at the same time. Educators need to meet them at their level. One child's brain might be developing faster with specific language skills, while another seems to be excelling with spatial abilities. Educators must help them find their own way of accomplishing developmentally appropriate tasks, inspire them, and allow for success. Children need to believe they can accomplish life's tasks.

Children's need for boundaries, structure, and expectations is another area undermined in many schools. School rules must be clear, consistent, and reasonable, but they also must be *flexible* enough to allow each child to be responsible for his/her own learning. Our schools consistently get so hung up on problems of conduct that the main focus of education is lost. As a result many children across our nation do not understand that getting an education requires that they fully participate in the educational process. Believing children want to learn and sparking that desire requires that we allow children to be more responsible for their learning.

The need for stable, supportive communities and cultural continuity applied to schools means children need to feel they are a part of their school community. They need to feel a sense of belonging in terms of their individual gifts, cultural heritage, and their individuality. Additionally, the schools need to fit in the larger community. Unfortunately, many schools have a toxic environment: unfit for healthy relationships or dynamic learning.

The final basic need implies that all involved with children assist them with nurturing self-respect and self-acceptance, which is the first step for encouraging respect and tolerance for others. As educators, we need to begin by accepting each child, helping to grow healthy self-respecting individuals who value and respect the rights of all others, and who see the need for differences and celebrate the diversity of others.

Although most of our schools today allow children of all races and nationalities to participate academically, I believe the need for self-respect and tolerance of differences goes much deeper than ethnicity. All too often only lip service is given to this need in our schools. Rarely is true diversity really celebrated: the respect and celebration of the creative uniqueness of all individuals. Instead the focus seems to be more on expecting children to be more the same, to learn at the same rate, in the same manner, to behave the same way, and to not upset the apple cart with too many questions.

It seems clear that safe and productive schools must meet all the basic needs, and doing so will benefit all individuals involved in our schools: students, teachers, administrators, staff, parents and the community. Meeting these basic needs should be a starting point for all those interested in developing a positive school climate.

We also must learn from the mistakes of previous educational movements including the Self-esteem Movement. To have esteem for one's self is a valuable attribute, but self-esteem cannot be given or taught to students. Self-esteem does not come from teachers always praising the students, but instead from students working hard and succeeding. False self-esteem, praising students when they know they are not doing well only helps to promote a lack of trying. Threatening children that they will not get into the college of their choice or never get a decent job only makes kids give up in frustration. So much of what happens in schools in the name of trying to motivate students to do their best actually backfires and creates a climate of pessimism.

Martin Seligman (1995) offers a much more useful and hopeful approach to assisting students to understand and take responsibility for how they feel and think about themselves. Seligman sees self-esteem as a mental state or a way in which the child explains his/her successes and failures to himself. If the child understands who is responsible, he/she can then take more accountability for his/her learning. If the child understands that there is something he can do about his situation and that it will not have lifelong consequences then the child can have a more optimistic outlook, will be less apt to give up, and more likely to take responsible steps toward making his situation better.

No Child Left Behind, with all its good intentions, created an atmosphere of even more pessimism. The strong focus on accountability and test scores overlooked the needs of children, particularly the needs to engage individual differences and developmentally appropriate programs.

We can learn a lot from Martin Seligman about developing schools which are conducive to learning and are emotionally resilient. Dr. Seligman (1998) believes that we can and should teach our administrators, teachers and students to be optimistic.

Failure can and will occur in school even when talent and desire are present if there is not an optimistic perspective present. Along with this, children must be taught the important life messages of not giving up, mastering frustration and challenges.

Additionally, schools today are rushing children to grow up quicker, to comprehend concepts at earlier ages, and to behave as pint-sized adults at the expense of their childhood. According to David Elkind, this trend does not result in greater learning for the children, but does put added stress on already overburdened children. Attempting to speed up children's learning can result in a weak academic foundation. Children do not understand many concepts at early ages. Therefore, material needs to be presented with a solid underlying foundation, which is all too often shaky when we hurry learning.

We also must consider the groundbreaking work of Dr. Howard Gardner and the applications his theory has when applied to issues of school climate. Multiple Intelligence Theory can be very helpful in establishing a nurturing, thriving, safe school climate! (MI Theory looks at the following forms of intelligences: linguistic, logical-mathematical, musical, bodily-kinesthetic, spatial, interpersonal, intrapersonal, naturalistic, and even possibly existential and spiritual; Gardner, 1999).

We now know from school climate research that an optimal learning setting is one that understands, accepts, and respects individual needs and differences. By incorporating the theory of multiple intelligences and viewing each child in terms of his/her unique intelligences, we are able to obtain a fuller understanding of the child and to nurture each child's unique strengths while helping to develop areas which may be weaker. We also know that traditional intelligence tests do not show an adequate picture of an individual's unique intelligences. Furthermore, many children do not test well, and are discriminated against as a result. We'll learn more about this in Chapter 5.

Now that we have established a solid footing for our foundation, let's take a closer look at how these cutting edge researchers and practitioners help us to further our understanding of improving school climates. The viewpoints of Brazelton, Greenspan, Levine, Gardner, and Seligman, discussed above, fit well with the six elements in my definition of school climate presented in chapter one. School climate refers to a unique *balance* of intellectual, behavioral, social, ethical/moral, and physical characteristics of a school.

1. *Intellectual Element:* Without question, academics need to be a major focus in the mission of all schools. However, schools with hidden dangers are overly focused on test scores, comparison and ranking of students, and a rigidity to learning. Safe, productive schools have high academic expectations for their students, observe individual learning styles, and focus on depth and application of learning. It is essential to fully understand the unique individual differences and to know how to bridge the gap from research to education when working with children.

   Furthermore, Dr. Howard Gardner and his Multiple Intelligence approach considers viewing each child's unique combination of intelligences as being much more respectful, and less damaging to the child's self-concept, than is diagnosing. Children are not seen as deficient or labeled, but valued for their uniqueness (Gardner, 1999). Only then may students believe in themselves; to understand they can succeed academically.

2. *Behavioral Element:* All schools may experience problems of school disorder from time to time. School disorder includes issues of school violence, victimization, avoidance, perceptions of safety, and misconduct. According to Welsh (2000) research on school climate offers significant potential for understanding and preventing school violence. (p.88)

   Issues of school disorder and violence are on the minds of most parents today and are a concern for many students as well. Yet, it is how these problems are handled which determine safe and productive conditions. In schools with hidden dangers these issues may be handled with little regard for consistency. Bullying tactics may be inadvertently reinforced by attitudes which perceive the victims as weak or in need of "toughening up," problem students may be unintentionally given preferential treatment, and victimized students may not be heard with their silent cries for help. Additionally, living with the possibility of terrorist attacks and the heightened awareness of the volatile world events, students' perceptions of safety must be worked through. Furthermore, according to the research of McEvoy and Welker (2000) antisocial behavior must be viewed from a broader perspective and include research on academic failure and school climate.

   If we focus too narrowly on the individual as having the only problem, then ineffective interventions will continue. If on the other hand we begin to modify the climate where academic failure and antisocial behavior occur, then effective changes can take place and will benefit all.

In safe, productive schools these same problems are present, yet the problems are faced head on in an open, consistent and fair manner. Teacher, staff, student, parent and community concerns are *genuinely* heard and addressed.

3. *Emotional Element:* This element takes into consideration how those involved with schools feel about their school and themselves. Are children and teachers feeling anxious, depressed, or pessimistic about their day-to-day work? Possibly it is their perspective that may be contributing to these negative states. Certainly I am not suggesting schools alone are responsible for increased levels of anxiety and depressive disorders; but I am suggesting that certain problems and issues could be approached differently in the schools to help develop a positive optimistic climate. We know from the research of Martin Seligman (1998) that we can and should teach our administrators, teachers and students to be optimistic. Seligman believes that failure can and will occur in school even when talent and desire are present if an optimistic perspective is not present.

4. *Social Element:* All schools develop a unique social aspect. In toxic schools teachers, students, and parents may not feel as if they belong, or as if they are valued and appreciated. There is little sense of community in such schools.

    In the best schools a positive sense of community exists. Students, teachers and administrators feel they fit in and are making a positive contribution. It is not unusual to see older students helping younger students and accepting responsibility for the well-being of their schools and classmates. In safe, productive schools there is a definite sense of belonging. Teacher, student and parental input are all welcomed and seen as a genuine and valuable contribution. (Hoy and Woolfolk)

5. *Ethical/Moral Element:* This element can be determined by answering the question: Are we doing good work? Good work is defined by Gardner, Csikszentmihalyi, and Damon (2001) as involving excellence and ethics. When excellence and ethics are in harmony we can lead a personally fulfilling and socially rewarding life while doing good work.

Hoy and Woolfolk (1993) have studied teachers'sense of efficacy and the relationship to the organizational health of schools. They believe that typically, teachers do not have the background or experience to handle day-to-day tasks in the classroom. According to Hoy and Woolfolk (1993) inexperienced—and many experienced—teachers do not have a solid grasp of the psychological and learning theories to implement effective teacher/learning environments. Furthermore, teachers are asked to teach children with severe emotional, behavioral, physical, and learning disorders. Nowhere in their background have they been trained to handle these problems. Hoy and Woolfolk (1993) believe that beginning teachers must have additional coursework, time, support and supervision to feel a positive sense of efficacy. Fifteen years later Hoy and Woolfolk's findings are still accurate.

We also must ask other questions of ourselves. Are we doing the best we can for each child . . . adjusting to the uniqueness of each child, looking not for what is wrong, but celebrating the strengths of the individual?

In schools with hidden dangers such questions are not readily asked. There appears to be a passivity on the part of those involved in the schools and therefore practices do not change. In the best schools we see educators encouraged to question, to seek alternatives, to do their best work.

6. *Physical Element:* Last, but certainly not least, we must consider the influence of physical setting on the health of the school community. We have known from many years of teaching that the arrangement of desks, the colors on the walls, the size of the windows all have an impact of the climate of a setting. More recently, we have become aware of research in the medical field that other factors may also have an impact on health and ability to learn. These factors may include, but are not limited to, the food served in the cafeterias, undetected mold and environmental hazards that interfere with learning, and the health of those exposed. (NCEF Resource List: National Clearinghouse for Educational Facilities)

When students and teachers are continually exposed to conditions that are unhealthy they will not be able to do their best work. Indeed, many children's apparent hyperactivity, learning problems, and health issues may be resolved just by moving them to a physically healthy setting. Certainly, it would be unfortunate for such a child to suffer the consequences of misdiagnosis and needless medication when the building was the problem; and all children, faculty and staff would benefit by needed repairs/renovations.

Clearly, a safe and productive school climate involves a unique balance of the intellectual, behavioral, social, ethical/moral, and physical elements of a school. Addressing these basic elements will benefit all individuals involved in our schools: students, teachers, administrators, staff, parents and the community and should be a starting point for all those interested in developing a positive school climate.

Along with reviewing research, consulting with teachers, administrators, pediatricians, school counselors, school nurses, community members and most importantly the children and the parents is essential! Doing so can lead to a more complete understanding of the school's total environment. So, consult I did. Over many years, I have talked with teachers, doctors, administrators, school psychologists, school counselors, community members, and of course many parents and their children.

I wanted to know what characteristics and conditions are believed to have caused problems for the children and what characteristics and conditions are important to have a healthy milieu. The answers are informative and go even deeper than the issues described in the brief case of Kevin. The information gathered gets at the very heart of the problems inherent in the hidden dangers within our schools, and reveals the essentials for developing thriving, safe school environments.

There are thousands of kids floundering in our schools, and so not developing into the people they have the potential to become. Educating our children is our most important job as adults; helping them to become all they are capable of becoming and to grow into the people they were meant to become. Yet it seems we are stifling the very essence out of our children and robbing them of the education they deserve.

The next several chapters will look in depth at specific hidden dangers within our schools, ones I have discovered from my work with educators, parents, students, and as a parent myself. We'll begin in Chapter 3 by looking at the hidden danger of out-dated and distorted attitudes, beliefs and procedures.

> Teachers pass on the important information of the past and prepare their students for the future.
>
> —Gardner, Csikszentmihalyi, & Damon, (2001, p. 10)

Chapter 4

Misguided Assumptions, Attitudes, and Procedures that Negatively Impact Smart Kids

"More important than the curriculum is the question of methods of teaching and the spirit in which the teaching is given."

—Bertrand Russell

Sometimes the attitudes, beliefs, and procedures which have become so ingrained in the schools just do not "fit," explain, or help all children and they may be negatively impacting your child's education. There are many hidden assumptions, attitudes and procedures that occur routinely in schools without much thought or analysis. One possible explanation for this occurrence is that we become comfortable with familiar routines. We believe we must being doing OK because that's the way schools have always operated. Another likely possibility involves a combination of factors including a lack of time, expertise, energy, or money to look thoughtfully into these issues; but there definitely is a need to do so!

Let's begin with looking at issues within our society. No doubt we live in a wonderful country. However, having freedom and a right to a free public education can have its dark side. Possibly we've grown to expect that education is something that is given to our students; a passive process, where many expect learning to be spoon fed to them. But a true education cannot be obtained in this manner. Education is a process which develops over time through hard work, dedication and perseverance. It is undeniably a right living in our country, but it is also truly a gift—one that must be earned.

All too often we see students doing only the bare minimum of work to get by in their classes. Our natural response to this is to blame them, to say they are lazy, unmotivated and even ungrateful. But they have learned these behaviors from their parents, from their teachers and from society. We cannot change this norm overnight, but we can make small changes within our schools to triumph over this self-defeating learned behavior. Change is difficult and often a slow process because of the significant resistance to change within many schools.

However, this resistance can be overcome if we acknowledge there is a problem, stop blaming, and change what we can. Yes, I know there are many problems in our society over which we have no control: poverty, violence, family issues to name a few, but there are also hidden resistances in our schools that, if identified, we can do something about!

One such hidden resistance is the assumption that if a child is not learning, then there must be something wrong with the child. Why are we reluctant to consider the possibility that the child might not be to blame? Well, I suspect it is the age old issue of human nature again. We all can become a bit defensive when we believe our work or our personhood is being attacked. However, this is a huge misunderstanding of the issues at hand. We do not need to feel defensive when some children are doing reasonably well in our classes. We should instead be asking the question, "What can we do differently so that struggling children and all children can do better?"

Ideally, it is best to address the issues of any child from a holistic perspective, including a complete analysis of the school's climate. Keep in mind that positive change in school climate will benefit all students, making school a safer and more productive place for all. However, a holistic analysis is not what usually happens. More often than not the struggling child is seen to have a "problem" that must be addressed, rather than asking what factors in the environment could possibly be interfering with the child's learning.

Resistance to change is natural; it is a part of our human nature. It is difficult to acknowledge that our beliefs, our policies, and the approaches that we've been trained to use might not always be best. However, I believe that most of us in the fields of education and psychology want to help the children with whom we work. Therefore, it is of the utmost importance that we be open-minded to the possibility that we need to question our policies and practices. We need to keep abreast of the current research in our fields, consult with professionals outside of our fields, and acknowledge our limitations. We need to look at all possible factors contributing to the problems we are seeing with our children in the schools.

Another hidden problem involves a faulty assumption based upon a misinterpretation of research which, in turn, has led to decades of misguided efforts to help children develop more positive self-esteem. The self-esteem movement noted in the previous chapter began back in the late 1960's with a research project done by Stanley Coopersmith (1967), a project that was misunderstood. Coopersmith, a psychologist, believed that raising children's self-esteem was important in proper child rearing. His results correlated well with age-old childrearing practices that require clear rules and enforced limits in order for children to develop higher self-esteem. (Cited in Seligman, 1995, pp. 27–28)

Unfortunately, many educators paid attention only to the feeling good part of boosting the child's self-esteem, lavishing praise on children for their work; even when children knew they weren't doing well, or putting forth their best efforts! Clearly this approach has backfired. Encouraging a false sense of self-esteem without putting in the hard work is a dangerous approach! Indeed, self-esteem decreases when children realize, as most of them do, that the praise they have received is unfounded.

Academic policies must be continually appraised and revised when needed. The case of Nathan portrays a good example of a problem that can occur from a misguided assumption. Nathan was in eighth grade and doing very little reading at home when his parents became concerned. Nathan was not a boy who liked to read for pleasure, although he was surrounded by books at home and his parents both were ardent readers. They believed that the manner in which reading assignments were approached during school time, and definitely for homework, were contributing to Nathan's lack of reading for pleasure! Nathan explained that he was required to read ten pages of a novel of his choice; then to stop and write a journal entry about what he had read. This approach was counterproductive to really getting into a page turner of a novel and not wanting to put the book down; it was very disruptive to the joy of reading!

Nathan was not even close to doing his best work, but his teacher was nonetheless commending his petty effort. So, Nathan's parent asked the teacher exactly what the assignment entailed. She reported that Nathan was correct in his understanding and that students were required to read only 70 pages over the course of the term! Now how can anyone learn to love to read when expectations are so low, and they have to stop every ten pages? No one is going to enjoy reading this way. Low expectations are a detrimental danger undermining all students' unrealized abilities—abilities which may remain concealed in such an environment!

The teacher's explanation of this absurd approach was that she didn't want the children who were poorer readers to feel badly! Students could always read more than assigned, but Nathan, like most boys his age, took the easy route . . . and was being harmed by this poorly thought out and dangerous process!

Then there is the case of Mark which helps to illuminate other hidden ideas and policies in the schools. Mark is a ten-year-old child from a typical household. Mom and Dad both work outside of the home, but Mom returns home at three o'clock in the afternoon to be available to her children. Mark has an older sister and one younger brother. He is active and engaged with learning in the classroom and gets along well with his classmates. After school Mark likes to relax for a while playing basketball in the driveway or riding his bike around the neighborhood. Like most boys his age he likes computer games, sports and watching television, although his parents limit the amount of time and the programs he is allowed to watch.

Mom and Dad are caring, involved parents that place a clear value on education. This case study sounds like an ideal supportive family and Mark sounds like a typical boy with strengths and talents in many areas. However, in school Mark developed the reputation of a child with hyperactivity and attention problems. His teacher strongly suggested that the boy should be put on Ritalin. Clearly this teacher was overstepping her bounds, having no credentials to diagnose ADHD or suggest the use of medication. Although this diagnosis was ruled out by his pediatrician and a psychologist, the label "stuck" within his school. It seems that in some schools there is an overabundance of children with a diagnosis . . . if not this diagnosis, then another; and children often become what we label them.

Unfortunately, this is not an unusual scenario. Many children are viewed as deficient or different because they learn differently, are not learning up to expectations, or they are not behaving as most other children. Sometimes an accurate diagnosis is helpful, but a misdiagnosis can be harmful. This mislabeling and misperception of the child is not done intentionally, but it frequently happens as a matter of routine without looking at other possible causes, because the child may exhibit some characteristic "symptoms" of a disorder. Nevertheless, the misunderstanding and overuse of diagnosis can be at tremendous cost to the child.

The school's motives are almost always well intended; school personnel do not want to overlook a treatable problem. However, are we in turn overlooking other possible causes of school difficulties by simply labeling (putting the blame) on the child and undermining the child's security and sense of self, when changes within the school may be all that is necessary? There are so many inherent dangers with diagnosing that we will look in-depth at these issues in chapter five.

Then there is the case of Sally. This case helps to clarify four other hidden procedural problems which could be identified early and corrected if we look at and accurately understand the symptoms of children who are experiencing school related anxiety. These issues include a lack of continuity, undertrained personnel, toxic testing, and overscheduling.

Sally's parents report that she was anxious in school. She got off to a difficult start in first grade when her teacher went on maternity leave and there were several temporary substitutes for the remainder of the school year. We know from chapter 3 that continuity is important, particularly to young children (Brazelton & Greenspan, 2000). Could this be causing some of Sally's anxiety? I have heard of a similar a problem when school systems went through a redistricting process, another procedure we should question. Some students are sent to a different school as a result, uprooted from friends and the comfortable familiarity of their previous neighborhood school, often paying a high emotional price for a policy based on anything but the child's needs!

By the second grade, Sally reported that she found it difficult to focus on her own work; she was worrying what might happen next. There were two children with severe behavior problems in her class. At times they threw chairs and other objects, and even hit other students. Naturally, these students required a lot of extra time from the classroom teacher who was not trained to handle behavioral problems of this proportion. Sally often sat under her desk when things got out of control in the classroom. Here is the hidden dilemma related to teachers not having adequate training and expertise to know how to handle children with severe emotional and behavioral problems.

We certainly wouldn't allow a surgeon to operate without proper credentials and training. Yet we are entrusting the education and ultimately the futures of our children to individuals who lack adequate expertise. Most teachers would welcome additional education and training. They want to help children and they take their jobs seriously. For the most part teachers are not the problem.

Of course we should mention two serious problems at this point. We should be encouraging the best and brightest of our college students to become teachers. But many of our talented young adults go into other fields where they are able to command higher salaries. Teachers are underpaid. Another problem involves the tenure policies which allow poor teachers to stay at their jobs, collect their pay checks, and rob children of the education they deserve! And we reward our best teachers by having them teach children who will learn anyway.

A quote from Hillary Clinton clearly articulates this problem:

> "Merit pay to individual teachers would discourage teachers from helping troubled students and would create a distorted competition among teachers. I don't think that's a very good way to inspire teachers. We want our best teachers to work with the kids who are the hardest to teach. If teachers are going to be told that the people who look better on a test are the ones who are going to get them rewarded in salary or compensation, why would anyone take on the kids who are harder to teach?" (New York Times, April 6, 2000, p. 25)

Furthermore, we must question the policy of tenure of teachers. Currently schools get stuck keeping teachers who have lost their enthusiasm, and others who clearly are incompetent or not dedicated to their profession, and in some cases even harmful to the learning process of children. Such teachers need to be given a chance to change and improve their approaches, but should not be allowed to remain negatively impacting the education of children year after year. Yes, it is important to have some degree of security in one's job; but there also needs to be the motivation and ability to consistently do good work. In such a positive school climate both the teachers and the students benefit.

Over time our nation's schools have been expected to take on more roles and responsibilities. These additional tasks are ones for which classroom teachers have not been adequately prepared or fairly compensated. Teachers are expected to be the jack of all trades. Many school systems respond by putting a teacher's aide in the classroom. The aide is usually an individual with little or no training! This response makes no sense at all and at best can only be seen as a band aid approach to a serious problem!

By third grade Sally was exhibiting other concerns related to performance anxiety. Third grade was the year all students take standardized achievement tests and her teacher was stressing the importance of these instruments. Testing has taken on far too much importance in our schools. The hidden dangers of testing need a chapter of their own and will be analyzed in-depth in chapter 4.

Additionally, Sally was overscheduled with after school programs including drama, soccer, and music lessons. (Readers may want to refer to: "The Hurried Child," by Dr. David Elkind.) Yet her school required her participation in many extended day activities and graded her participation on her report card. There was even some required weekend participation! Sports, music, and other formerly relaxing activities became a competitive, compulsory grind.

Even looking at a typical day's academic schedule should get us thinking. Students are required to change subjects every 45–50 minutes (younger children even more often). The rationale behind this hectic schedule involves the idea that children cannot maintain attention for longer periods of time . . . but this is an inaccurate belief and a faulty approach for many learners. They can easily get back to the tasks at hand and learn in more depth if they are not required to stop and change classes and subjects when they are engrossed in learning.

Arbitrary time restraints are ludicrous and this includes times for lunch, bathroom breaks and other basic needs. Kids should be allowed to address their basic needs when necessary. For example, it's very difficult for many students to think in class right before lunch when they haven't eaten since early morning. Even adults are allowed a coffee break mid morning!

In classes that end at the bell, students are anticipating this event and often have long before shut down to learning. These barriers to learning are very disruptive to all students, particularly those who learn in depth. Many students cannot turn off their thinking in one subject; they do not quickly gear up for art or history when still deep in thought about a math problem or a concept that sparked their interest in the previous class . . . and it is wrong to interrupt this thought process!

We also should look at some of the interpretation of the laws developed to protect the children's right to education. Terms like "least restrictive environment," "mainstreaming," and "inclusion" are meant to protect children from being discriminated against, allowing children with special needs to be integrated in regular classrooms. This of course is a good idea . . . most of the time. But there are definitely times when a regular classroom cannot provide the education some children may require to "not be left behind"!

Teachers cannot be experts in all areas and we are doing a disservice by not placing students with those having expertise in dealing with specific issues. It may be best for a child who is experiencing severe learning difficulties to be placed in a specialized school for a year or two so that the child can be taught in the manner in which he/she learns best. Then the student can be integrated back into the mainstream, self-esteem intact, with skills to thrive academically. Teachers should be chosen for each child based upon the child's needs, not upon which classroom has space.

Another idea might allow a parent to switch the child's class or school when there is a failure to thrive in an academic setting. Sometimes just a change in schools is all that is needed if it is a change to a school with a better "fit" for the child. It's not unusual for a child to be receiving poor grades and experiencing numerous problems because of a school setting. The special education team may be called in, searching for problems (with the child, the parents, or even society), when all that may be needed is a change in school environment.

Then there is the issue of the number of students in each class. Well-documented research clearly shows there is a correlation between smaller numbers and higher levels of achievement. Large classrooms require teachers to teach in different ways too. It's much more difficult to conduct experiments, debates, and seminars with large classes. Lecture is the more typical approach, but will not meet the needs of many students. In the early grades teachers often use many worksheets; sometimes it is to reinforce learned material, but sometimes it is just busywork to keep large classes under control.

Carol's story is a good example of the effects of this dysfunctional approach. She is an only child of an intact professional family. Carol began hating school by third grade; she continually complained that school was boring and that the work was the same day after day. According to Carol and her parents, there were far too many worksheets. These were seen as an attempt to keep the children busy in a classroom with too many students, many with problems too difficult for the teacher to handle. Although there was a teacher's aide in the classroom, this aide had no educational background or training. Typical children were not thriving in this setting. Research backs up the premise that smaller classes do make a difference.

Homework is another area that needs to be looked into. Certainly homework is necessary at times to reinforce learning which occurred during the day. However, it seems that more and more homework is being assigned because of arbitrary homework policies (for example high school students should do 2 hours of homework a night). Such policies need to be revised. Most homework is only busy work which frustrates and turns kids off to school. Time could be much better spent relaxing with family, reading a good book, or with sports.

The age-old issue of grading, progress reports, and report cards is another policy that needs revamping. Students so often get far too much negative feedback, become anxious, or worse yet, stop caring. Chad is a young student suffering from the ill effects of this policy. Chad's mother was sent weekly "progress reports," but noted that only negative comments were reported . . . never any positive comments even though this is a bright, academically successful child. Grades were intended to motivate students and inform them of their growth. Instead they have too often become a form of punishment with all the harmful ramifications.

Discipline and behavior management issues are far too much of a problem for all schools. In fact, I believe that there is so much of a focus on what kids might do wrong, that many kids are beginning to think that it is the norm to act in an inappropriate manner! Clearly, all teens do not act irresponsibly all of the time. Many teens do not experience periods of storm and stress as the media seems to portray. We need to start expecting that children can and will act responsibly.

Along these same lines, children need to be given more responsibility for their learning, have choices in what they want to learn and how they want to learn it. We need to trust that they want to learn, that they want to do the right thing and will behave in their best interest . . . at least most of the time. Many of our current educational policies on discipline and behavior are counterproductive to the mission of the schools to teach children to become responsible, knowledgeable individuals. (Our new school safety policies will be addressed in depth in chapter 8.

One parent expressed her concerns regarding the inflexibility of the manner in which students were handled when disciplinary issues did arise. She described her child's school as having only one way of dealing with problems, a very inflexible way. They don't allow for individual differences.

Another parent, the mother of David, expressed her thoughts about the poor handling of discipline problems. The school's policies were reported as inconsistent and ineffective. For example, one boy was frequently out of control in the classroom and there was an incident involving physical violence. The aggressive child was spoken to in the principal's office and then sent back to class with no other consequences or follow up. There are numerous stories when serious discipline problems were not handled appropriately.

This same parent volunteered in the classroom and observed other problems. She expressed concern that the children with obvious behavioral problems were being rewarded for their inappropriate actions. She noticed that in special classes such as music and gym, these children were allowed to use the drums or their choice of musical instrument just so there wouldn't be an incident. She spoke of children with severe behavioral and emotional disorders taking all of the teachers' time and energy at the expense of the other children. The regular kids were being left out and falling through the cracks.

It also appears that boys are often in time out or other forms of disciplinary measures much more often than girls in school settings. This phenomenon should get us wondering why this is the case. Are boys not ready for school, do boys have more behavioral problems? Are there gender expectations in our schools that are not realistic? There are behavioral differences between the genders, and little boys should not be made to feel as if they are "bad" because they act differently than girls. Girls usually have a much easier time with rules in the schools setting. I'm not saying that we should overlook or excuse the inappropriate behavior of some boys, nor should we throw up our hands and give up, ranting the platitude, "boys will be boys"... But possibly we should understand boys better and change the school climate so it is more conducive to them.

Then there are the issues involved with the "tone" or attitude of the administration, faculty and staff. In many schools this tone is pleasant, welcoming and affirming. However, there are schools where even the parents feel threatened, almost as if they are children again themselves and have been called down to the principal's office. In such schools, communication is not welcomed and parental involvement is not encouraged. These are closed schools where the attitudes are authoritarian and non-democratic. There is no room for negotiation or reflection upon their own assumptions, attitudes, or procedures.

One parent summed up her thoughts succinctly about such a setting. She believed the tone was set by the upper administration and if nothing was done the problems would indeed perpetuate. She understood that in her child's system the superintendent backed up the principal, the principal backed up the teachers, and the teachers backed up the staff, but there was no one to listen to the parents or the students. In the case of one child, I'll call her Becky, emotional harm was caused from an unkind lunchroom staff woman, who spoke angrily and in a demeaning manner to the students. Becky was so fearful she at first was not able to eat and soon she and her friends skipped lunch altogether rather than encounter this paid bully. Poor eating habits have developed. (Bullies aren't always the kids!) Unfortunately, no one listened to these children or to the parents. The same personnel and policies remained.

We must also consider the timing of the school day. Research study after research study documents that, during adolescence, natural sleep cycles change so that children stay awake later and need to sleep later in the mornings. Unfortunately most high schools start very early; 7:30 AM and even earlier is not unusual, which means many adolescents are getting up by 5:30–6:00 AM or earlier to finish homework and get on the school bus. However, adolescents need at least 8–9½ hours of sleep per night or they will be at an increased risk of depression and attention issues, along with a decrease in learning; not to mention a higher risk of car accidents for those sleepy students who have their driver's license. So what do the schools do? They start the academic day earlier and earlier . . . not based upon research which clearly states what is best for the child . . . but based upon a budget issue. School buses cost money and the high school students must get up and start early so that the younger children can then be picked up and brought to their schools.

Even basic policies on eating and exercise needed reviewing. Children need nutritious food and need it more often than adults. Many children need to eat several smaller healthy meals throughout the day. Yet the school schedule does not allow for this need. According to the professionals at the Mayo Clinic, children, unlike adults, need extra nutrients and calories to fuel their growth and development. (Mayo Clinic, 2006)

Many children are unable to focus, particularly in the class right before lunch, because their need for food is more urgent than anything the teacher might be attempting to teach. When children are allowed to pay attention to their bodies' needs they learn to eat when needed and not when they are not hungry. If children were allowed nutritious snacks during the morning hours, if and when needed, many children would be more alert and not craving the high fat and sugary temptations that are the target of many in need of quick energy. (Parents and educators also should be aware that food additives and food colorings can interfere with some very sensitive children's ability to focus and learn. Since such additives do not have a nutritious value they should be avoided by all children.)

When lunchtime finally arrives, children typically have twenty to twenty-five minutes for lunch which includes standing in line to obtain their lunches. Usually there are only a few minutes to gulp down a few bits; the rest is dumped into the trash. Lunchtime needs to be relaxed, allowing time for socialization and a break from the academic routine. Nutritious selections must be all that is accessible for children, along with adequate time for consumption. Several tempting choices should be readily available including healthy main courses and desserts.

The incidence of childhood obesity has grown rapidly in this country for many reasons. We live in an industrialized nation where fast foods are a way of life for many, offering convenience, availability, and attraction to children through aggressive advertising campaigns. According to research from the Mayo Clinic, in just two decades, the prevalence of overweight children has doubled in the United States for youth aged 6 to 11. The obesity rate has tripled for American teenagers. Furthermore, the annual National Health and Nutrition Examination Survey by the Centers for Disease Control and Prevention found that about one-third of United States children are overweight or at risk of becoming overweight. In totality, it appears that approximately 25 million United States children and adolescents are now considered overweight. (Mayo Clinic, 2006)

Although there are some genetic causes for childhood obesity, most is the result of poor choices of food, too much food, and the decrease in activity levels. Our sedentary lifestyle is on the rise and schools need to address the changing times. Clearly, technology has advanced the potential for educational advancement and most kids enjoy and excel in the use technology. Yet it does also decrease the amount of time kids are engaged in active pursuits.

Amazingly enough, the trend in education has been to ignore this need for increased activity level, by cutting down on the required hours and days during which children must be involved in physical education. Particularly at the middle schools and high school levels, adolescents are required to take only one term of physical education per year! Even in elementary schools, recess times are few and far between in the faulty belief that academic time is being wasted if kids are out running around. In truth kids are able to focus better when their need for physical activity is addressed . . . particularly those who may be misdiagnosed as having attention problems!

Even the physical layout of the school building and classrooms needs to be considered. The products used in building, renovations and upkeep are also problematic in many of our nation's schools. When new schools are being constructed careful planning must go into the specifications and include information from architects and builders, along with research from the fields of education, psychology and medicine to address these concerns. These concerns warrant a chapter of their own and will be addressed in chapter 9.

This chapter has looked at some of the school issues that are the most troublesome, where assumptions, attitudes, and procedures are determined and implemented in the name of education. Many other countries do not have the same issues in their schools. We need to ask ourselves why so many of our children do not want to go to school, why they do not value a good education. Even

Figure 4.1. Hidden Dangers Vicious Cycle

those who do manage to graduate from high school are very often ill-prepared to deal with the academic rigor they encounter when attending college!

It has not always been this way in our country, and we can make changes to improve the quality of education before more harm is done. We'll see all of these hidden themes emerge again in a variety of circumstances and cases as we look in-depth at specific hidden dangers. It is helpful to keep the following Hidden Dangers Vicious Cycle in mind as we go through the following chapters.

> It is, in fact, nothing short of a miracle that the modern methods of instruction have not yet entirely strangled the holy curiosity of inquiry; for this delicate little plant, aside from stimulation, stands mainly in need of freedom; without this it goes to wrack and ruin without fail. It is a grave mistake to think that the enjoyment of seeing and searching can be promoted by means of coercion and a sense of duty.
>
> —Albert Einstein

Chapter 5

The Hidden Dangers in Testing that Impact Your Child

> "Our students are tested to an extent that is unprecedented in American history and unparalleled anywhere in the world. Politicians and businesspeople, determined to get tough with students and teachers, have increased the pressure to raise standardized test scores. Unfortunately, the effort to do so typically comes at the expense of more meaningful forms of learning."
>
> —Alfie Kohn

My reason for writing this chapter on hidden dangers of testing began back in my early undergraduate years when a college professor from the field of Educational Psychology disclosed his personal history. When he was in kindergarten he had been administered an intelligence test on which he performed quite poorly. Based upon the test results he was placed in a residential school for the mentally retarded. One young woman recognized after some time that this child was not quite like the others; indeed he seemed to be quite bright. Fortunately for him this woman was able to get him out of the institution and back into a school where he thrived. This young boy grew up and later continued on to Harvard University from which he received his doctoral degree!

Well, one might say that this was many years ago and could never happen today. Unfortunately, we are still harming children with the effects of toxic testing in our schools. Our schools are caught up in a testing obsession that has its roots in the accountability movement of earlier decades. Don't get me wrong, being accountable is a good thing, and student learning should be measured and documented; but how we are determining students' learning is the problem. We're putting too much confidence in tests and the scores are often interpreted as an accurate reflection of a student's knowledge, skills, and abilities. Many students do not perform well on certain types of tests.

Testing in and of itself is a neutral process; it is when testing is misused that it can become quite a dangerous process. I have been involved with assessing students' learning for many years now. Earlier in my career I was involved with diagnosing students with learning disabilities and other disorders. After years of using tests to measure, diagnose, and establish appropriate educational plans, I have done a 180 degree turn in my viewpoint on the usefulness and effectiveness of many traditional tests. In fact, I see many assessment approaches as being imprecise and even damaging for many students!

Scott is one such student who was misunderstood on numerous school assessment instruments. He is an easygoing thirteen-year-old who is a delight, but has often times been a puzzle to his parents and teachers. He is a conscientious student who, overall, still likes school. He did very well on classroom work, easily followed the lectures and activities, although at times he got teachers off track with his insatiable curiosity and unique spin on classroom discussions. He seems to know a lot about many subjects and is inquisitive about most topics.

Scott has a few close friends, no diagnosed learning difficulties, and several intense interests. Math, science, foreign languages and history are his favorites. So what is the problem one might ask? Well, Scott is one of those bright, creative students who do poorly on standardized multiple choice tests, despite good grades and accelerated classes!

Students like Scott are plentiful in our schools; many students know more than they are able to demonstrate on traditional tests. A "one-size-fits-all" approach to testing is doomed to failure because of numerous imbedded problems with our current approach. In order to get to a fuller understanding of the hidden testing dilemmas we need to step back in time and look briefly at specific historical precedents in the fields of psychology and education.

HISTORICAL PERSPECTIVE

Testing and evaluation procedures have been a part of educated society for hundreds of years and individual abilities have been recognized since the dawn of history. The first tests were designed by the ancient Chinese around 2200 BC. Plato and Aristotle wrote on individual differences as far back as 2500 years ago. Many of the earliest tests used were oral examinations and presented the definite biases unique to this approach. (Aiken, 2000)

By the late 1800's and early 1900's testing was beginning to take on a more prominent role in the general public. In 1904, Alfred Binet was asked to develop the first intelligence test to weed out children who would not benefit from traditional schools in Paris, France (Aiken, 2000). Thus one of the first credible intelligence tests was born . . . although Binet was fully aware of the fallibility of the test scores. Certainly, this approach does not meet our needs today where all children are entitled to an education, but such tests are still in use in revised versions, although scores may be no more accurate or useful than a century ago.

We must also understand that early psychological theory was closely related to philosophy and understanding the world through a qualitative methodological approach. Understanding the experience was essential, during the late 1800's in Germany, Wilhelm Wundt started the ball rolling towards developing research approaches that would allow for quantifiable results. Measuring results became the theme for the next century and has continued on into current times, which is a good idea when used wisely. Proper assessment means using both qualitative and quantitative methodologies to fully understand the phenomenon being considered.

However, the field was moving quickly ahead, caught up in a trend of obsessively quantifying results without maintaining the more subjective (and at times deeper) understanding of the phenomena being studied. In the United States during the late 1940's and 1950's psychology was swept up in the behavioral era. B. F. Skinner and numerous other psychologists and educators were over-involved in the desire to make everything measurable. Unfortunately, the outcome was that people put more credence in these numbers than was healthy and forgot about the importance of measuring both qualitatively and quantitatively!

Significant historical and political developments also brought about change in testing needs. For example, both World War I and World War II caused an increased need for innovative approaches to test many recruits in a short period of time. Then came the race to get the first man in space and the first man on the moon which had a domino effect resulting in a frenzied attempt to increase student learning in math and science. One might cite this as the beginning of an *Academic Olympics* between the industrialized countries of the world. Thus the big business of testing was born along with an increased fervor for competition in academics!

These earlier attempts at testing seem to have established a mold which has been difficult to break. The pattern seems to address the style needs and thinking strategies of many students, but does not adequately address the needs of all. In fact, I think it is fair to question whether we are accurately measuring the true abilities of any student!

TODAY'S PERSPECTIVE

Psychologists and educators know that it is wrong to make decisions based upon a single test score; decisions should be based upon a balanced, complete understanding of each child. Numbers and scores can be very misleading if we don't consider the whole picture which means using both qualitative and quantitative approaches. Yet due to economic, time, and political pressures psychologists and educators are forced to rely more and more heavily on solely quantitative methods and many have been deceived into believing numbers tell the whole story.

Across the country we have a continued movement toward more accountability, increased use of standardized tests and high-stakes testing. Along with these trends come the negative symptom of teaching to the test, test anxiety, lowered self-esteem, misunderstandings of children, and missed opportunities for many. Dr. David Elkind, author of *The Hurried Child*, believes our current testing obsession is a factor behind the dynamics of our hurrying schools. Administrators are under pressure to demonstrate student learning and therefore are teaching concepts at earlier and earlier ages. This results in no greater knowledge, but added pressure for our children to measure up and to hurrying up their learning.

Very few countries in the world use standardized testing with children before the age of 16 years. But in the United States we use such tests with very young children even though we know this is contradictory to research findings and recommendations. Furthermore, very few countries use multiple choice formats with any age child. (Kohn, 2000)

Deborah Meier (2002) believes that this increase in the use of standardized tests actually undermines student achievement and increases the distrust many have for teachers, students, and their own judgments. The misunderstanding of testing develops into toxic conditions for everyone that is affected by test scores: students, teachers, parents, administrators, and the entire school system and community. We know from research that there is no one test that can determine a student's ability or achievement. Nor is there a test that can measure a teacher's or school system's effectiveness. To use tests in this manner is a flagrant misuse of testing, yet this is exactly what is happening!

Much of this drive toward greater accountability is fueled by political platforms. However, our well-meaning politicians are not trained in the art and science of testing, and many are influenced by the huge testing industry. Our children's education is too important to leave assessment decisions in the hands of those who do not comprehend the underlying issues in accurate assessment.

PROBLEMS WITH TRADITIONAL TESTING

Traditional tests attempt to show what a child does not know or what is wrong or deficient about a child's abilities, rather than what is valued and unique about the child's particular way of learning, coping, reasoning, or problem solving. Test developers are looking at assessment too narrowly. We need to break out of the mold of traditional assessment and develop assessment procedures which value and demonstrate the uniqueness of each individual.

Traditional testing is, at best, a selection of test items, which may or may not be relevant to the curriculum to which the student has been exposed and is always subject to many forms of bias including cultural, gender, socioeconomic and learning preference bias. Bias leads to assessment discrimination against many students including bright, creative, deep thinkers, students with learning differences, students with a preferred learning modality, boys due to gender differences, students from various ethnic and cultural backgrounds, and many students from lower socio-economic backgrounds. This is a lot of children!

So with all these children at risk, why are we so reliant on traditional testing approaches? Well, as I stated earlier, TESTING IS A BIG INDUSTRY, and the testing manuals advertise questionable advantages. For example, traditional standardized testing allows for: *standard practices and scoring* (the tests are given to all students in the same many and scored the same way). But, standardizing the process does not get rid of subjectivity. We are still making judgments, but in the case of most standardized testing instruments we are making judgments upon the lives of individuals with very little information. This is a very dangerous situation for many students!

Standardized testing also allows for *a comparison of students*. (however, when students are rank ordered the process assures that half will always be below average and the uniqueness of each student is often not seen). Such practices give a false illusion of being more scientific. Yet we know from the work of Brazelton and Greenspan (2000) that in order for children to learn and thrive we must meet their individual needs. We are not addressing individual needs with a one-size-fits-all approach to testing. There are many children with learning difficulties or just learning style differences. Most teachers do a good job of addressing these preferences in their teaching, but then we ignore the individual needs of most children when it comes to testing. We expect all children to be able to perform using one format. This is testing preference discrimination. Students should be allowed to demonstrate their competence in a way that shows what they really know and what they are capable of doing, while allowing their unique and often hidden abilities to shine through!

So with our current assessment strategies, kids like Scott with unique, idiosyncratic responses to test items are penalized. Their creative and deep-thinking approaches can actually handicap them on standardized tests. For example, a bright, creative student may come up with answers which may be correct, but are not the ones that the test designers had in mind.

Alfie Kohn (2000) gets this point across very succinctly. He believes there is a correlation between high scores on standardized tests and relatively shallow thinking, and that these kinds of tests are geared to a different, less sophisticated kind of knowledge (p. 9). Kohn (2000) goes on to say,

> "There are plenty of kids who think deeply and score well on tests. There are also plenty of students who do neither. But as a rule, good standardized test results are more likely to go hand in hand with a shallow approach to learning rather than with deep understanding." (p. 10)

Deborah Meier (2002) concurs that deeper and more subtle thought is often an impediment to scoring high on such tests.

Meier and Kohn are not alone in their beliefs about deep thinkers. Even back in 1962, B. Hoffman in the classic work, *The Tyranny of Testing*, demonstrates that these tests penalize the finer mind.

> He [the deep thinker] would see more in a question than his superficial competitors would ever dream was in it, and would expend more time and mental energy than they in answering it. That is the way his mind works. That is, indeed, his special merit. But the multiple choice tests are concerned solely with the candidate's choice of answer, not with his reason for his choice. Thus they ignore the elusive yet crucial thing we call quality. (p. 99)

Furthermore Hoffman states:

> Multiple choice format also penalizes the creative student. Students who can imagine several possible correct answers may think the most obvious answer could not be the correct answer (1962, p. 101).

One renowned psychologist remembers back to when he was a young child and actually suffered from the harmful effects of testing. Dr. Sternberg states:

> I did poorly on the tests and so, in the first three years of school, I had teachers who thought I was stupid and when people think you're stupid, they have low expectations for you . . . But my concern, given the relatively low predictability of the tests, is that there may be people who have tremendous talents, creative and practical talents, who, because they don't do well on these tests, never get the chance to show what they really could do in important jobs. (on-line interview)

Differences among socioeconomic levels and race have been well documented in the literature for having an effect on test scores. However, there are less well known issues of gender impacting standardized test scores. Dr. William Pollack (1998) believes that most of our schools are failing boys if they do not have an environment which is conducive to the way boys learn. Many schools do not and we are seeing a decline in boys' test scores as a result. Boys are often at a disadvantage on standardized multiple choice format tests, particularly in the earlier grades, due to subtle wording differences between items choices. Girls definitely have an advantage here.

W. J. Popham (1999) believes that educational quality is being measured by the wrong yardstick, and therefore, the evaluations are apt to be in error. He also believes that most educators as well as parents do not really understand the fact that standardized tests often provide misleading estimates of learning and of a school's effectiveness. So, many of these tests are being used for high-stakes decisions including student promotion or retention in grades, graduation, acceptance into certain schools, as well as judgments and punishments for the teacher . . . purposes for which the tests were not designed and which they cannot really do!

All this from tests that we know unfairly discriminate against a variety of students, show only a limited sample of behavior, presume similarity of educational content across classrooms, ignore individualizing ideas like progressivism and constructivism, make teachers and administrators narrow their curriculum to the test content and require teachers to focus more on test taking skills, thus losing valuable instruction time!

Furthermore, we are wasting taxpayers' money on these tests, rather than using needed funds for educational materials which would enrich all students. And most importantly, we are not getting an accurate picture of many of our students who may suffer humiliation and serious consequences from low scores.

It puzzles me how we can live in the most liberal country on earth, where the rights of the individual are prized and protected, yet with our approach to educational testing we expect everyone to demonstrate their learning in the same way. Because we are all individuals with different achievements, different learning styles, different backgrounds, and different response styles we must have a variety of testing formats if test takers are to accurately demonstrate their learning. We cannot tolerate a one-size-fits- all approach.

Of course we need high educational standards, but we need to be more reflective about our purposes for testing. Our purposes might include the need to pinpoint learning problems accurately in order to design appropriate educational programs, to improve the learning of all students, and to demonstrate that the children in our classrooms and schools are learning. In order to accomplish this goal of testing we need to develop more accurate assessment tools which do not have dangerous side effects.

We are definitely overusing and misusing a fallible method of assessment by relying so heavily on traditional standardized approaches. We can no longer afford to have such blind trust in a limited repertoire of assessment approaches. In order to break out of our current obsessive pattern of testing, we need innovative, motivated thinkers who know children well and realize the limitations of traditional tests, who are able to develop and fine-tune approaches that will measure learning over time, not just take a snapshot of a specific behavior at a specific point in time.

> I'm glad that the real world doesn't come with built-in multiple choice boxes, pre-coded and ready to score. (Meier, 2002, p. 181)

TOWARD A CONSTRUCTIVE SOLUTION

There are many ways to portray each child's distinctiveness more authentically. Alternative assessment approaches can portray each student's unique abilities and learning styles. For example, many teachers have been using a form of portfolio assessment for some time; some more effectively than others. It can be a time-consuming process, yet it has the added benefit of helping students to take responsibility for their learning and pride in their accomplishments.

Used well, portfolio assessment can demonstrate student learning, as well as students' strengths and weaknesses, and help to determine an appropriate learning program for each student (not just for a few identified students.). With further refinement this approach (combined with other qualitative and quantitative approaches) could be used to compare students' abilities and demonstrate the effectiveness of teachers' and educational programs' performance as well! Teachers will no longer be teaching to the tests, but looking toward what other, more ethical approaches to teaching and learning might benefit each child!

CASE STUDIES

Case studies can help illuminate these ideas. For example, the case of Noel is excellent to demonstrate the power of portfolio assessment. Noel experienced difficulty in early grades. Reading and writing did not come easily. She was diagnosed with a learning disability during third grade and was functioning below her peers in language arts despite high intelligence scores. Traditional tests did help to identify Noels' weaknesses, but were harmful to her in the manner they were used because her program focused on remediating her weaknesses and did not show up her numerous areas of academic talent. Her educational plan focused on the negative and did not allow the full child to develop. This was dangerous. Noel began to think of herself as less smart than her peers; self-esteem and self-confidence began to erode.

Test after test, year after year, her scores showed only her weaknesses. Noel developed a pessimistic outlook toward her future and felt trapped by a misleading approach to understanding her knowledge and skills. It wasn't until Noel reached college that she finally began to understand her strengths and value her abilities. Through portfolio assessment she demonstrated academic skills to herself, as well as her professors. She became a confident and competent young woman, graduating from college with honors and is now attending graduate school.

Noel was unique because she didn't give up. I suspect that many individuals have not persevered after test scores have put roadblocks in their way. (The current high school dropout statistics are alarming to say the least!) What a waste it is when human potential goes unrecognized, or, even more sadly, is misunderstood.

Then there is the case of Suzie. Suzie was always an excellent student who performed well on all standardized tests administered throughout her elementary and secondary school years. While in college she continued on this path toward success, clearly demonstrating her abilities as a scholar/athlete. Yet, with all the praise and glory, Suzie had been too narrowly focused on scores and competition. She did not understand all of her strengths, which are numerous. So, even in Suzie's case we did not get a complete picture of who this young woman might become.

When Suzie became involved with an evaluation process that required her to focus on her strengths and weaknesses, likes and dislikes, she discovered new talents and a balance to her life allowing more focused goals to emerge. Suzie was involved with experiential learning in her chosen field, trying out her knowledge and skills. This approach also allowed for outside objective professionals, as well as her professors, to evaluate her abilities. Suzie took responsibility for her learning and discovered artistic talents, strong interpersonal skills, and a desire and ability to help others. Clearly, by only focusing on scores, rank ordering each student, and what a child does not know, it is much too easy to lose sight of the individual and his or her potential! Portfolio assessment is just one approach we should be looking at more seriously for use with all students, not just the severely handicapped as is currently the practice.

To summarize: children should be taught that the purpose of testing is to help them review and more thoroughly learn material, to show them what they may still need to study a bit more, not to change possible options for their entire future! Teachers need to use testing to see what information they may need to readdress with students and can teach them to modify their teaching approaches accordingly. Testing should not be used to harm students or teachers. To misuse tests in such a manner quickly establishes a toxic and dangerous climate!

It is imperative that parents understand the appropriate use of testing, and even more importantly the misuses and limitations of testing, so they do not put too much credence in test scores which can harm their children.

> "So the question, for me, isn't if we ought to have some 'standards' in our children's education. It is, rather, how and where they are determined, and by whom, and how they're introduced, and how we treat or penalize (or threaten, or abuse) the child or teacher who won't swallow them."
>
> —Jonathan Kozol (2000, p. x)

Chapter 6

Hidden Dangers with Labeling that Can Harm Your Child

There is a brilliant child locked inside every student.

—Marva Collins

Marva Collins founded the Westside Preparatory School back in 1975 in an inner-city part of Chicago. Children were admitted to this school who had been labeled as problem children, learning disabled and even one child diagnosed as borderline mentally retarded. After only one academic year each student scored at least five grades higher proving that the previous labels placed on these children were inaccurate. Westside's graduates have gone on to many prestigious colleges and universities including Harvard, Yale and Stanford. These students are now professionals working as doctors, lawyers and educators. (Collins, M, Documented by CBS 60 Minutes, 1996)

Unfortunately, the more common scenario is for children who are labeled, or in some cases misdiagnosed, to not have an opportunity to be understood and allowed to develop their potential. Instead their potential has been crushed by the very labels that were supposed to help them!

Remember Kevin who we met in chapter one? He is a twelve year old pre-adolescent of at least above average intellectual ability, yet his school grades do not reflect his academic gifts. He wants to do well in school, but often does not complete assignments, study for exams, or even ask for help when needed. So what's going on with Kevin? Is he an unmotivated young man, or possibly ADHD or learning disabled? So often what happens in the schools is that professionals look to see what is wrong with the child who is not learning up to expectations, rather than looking at what might be wrong with the system, approach, teacher or classroom climate.

Unfortunately, this is not an unusual scenario. Many children are viewed as deficient or different because they learn differently, are not learning up to expectations, or are not behaving as most other children. Sometimes a child might indeed have a learning disability or other issue that interferes with learning, one which is in need of intervention. An accurate diagnosis can be an essential step toward getting the child the help he/she needs. So, it might be said that sometimes labeling is helpful, but often times children are overdiagnosed, misdiagnosed, and misunderstood which is harmful.

This mislabeling and misperception of the child is not done intentionally, but frequently happens as a matter of routine without looking at other possible causes, because the child may exhibit some characteristic "symptoms" of a disorder. However, the misunderstanding and overuse of diagnosis can be at tremendous cost to the child. The school's purpose is almost always well intended. School personnel do not want to overlook a treatable problem, but are they in turn overlooking other possible causes of school difficulties by simply labeling the child? Furthermore, are some educational professionals, at times, overstepping their levels of expertise when suggesting a child has a disorder?

These questions stuck in my mind as I sought to discover other possible causes of Kevin's "attention difficulties." (Many children do have true ADHD, but this diagnosis is being overused to label and treat children who are experiencing problems unrelated to a neurological difference.) So, let's take a closer look at Kevin. Kevin's parents report that he was anxious in school. He got off to a difficult start in first grade when his teacher went on maternity leave and there were several temporary substitutes for the remainder of the school year. We know that continuity is important, particularly to young children (Brazelton & Greenspan, 2000). Could this be causing some of Kevin's anxiety and increased activity level?

Kevin's mother was sent weekly progress reports during second grade, but noted that only negative comments were made; although this is a bright, academically successful child. Kevin needed to move around in his chair and periodically get up and walk around the classroom. Although this was against classroom rules it is clear that many boys need this type of flexibility and freedom from time to time. Unfortunately, Kevin was beginning to develop a negative self-concept, and did not enjoy going to school.

By third grade, Kevin reported that he found it difficult to focus on his own work while worrying what might happen next. There were two children with severe behavior problems in his class. At times they threw chairs and other objects, and even hit other students. Naturally, these students required a lot of extra time from the classroom teacher. Kevin often sat under his desk when things got out of control in the classroom.

Kevin reported not feeling safe or well cared for in this setting. He did experience difficulty paying attention in school, but not at home or elsewhere. Kevin's pediatrician helped rule out the diagnosis of ADHD. Certainly this is not a neurological problem, but a child who is a bit more aware that things were not quite right in his classroom. Instead of labeling Kevin, we could say he was demonstrating an adaptive response in order to cope in a setting that did not meet his needs. He was clearly aware that all was not well in his classroom.

Kevin also might be considered as a child who might be called a high reactor or if we wanted to we could possibly diagnose an anxiety disorder or some other disorder. But, would this be helpful . . . or harmful? I believe it would be harmful to Kevin. The term high reactor is really just another label for characteristics that we should be valuing, not looking at as a disorder. Kevin was born with an innate love of life, laughter, and creativity. Right from the beginning it was obvious to his parents that he was an unusual child; he was more alert, more aware and indeed more sensitive than most infants. Laughter came easily and early to this robust child. He enjoyed everything about the world, finding humor in most situations and he was interested in learning about everything.

Language too, was an early gift. It appeared to be a central driven force for Kevin to be able to communicate his thoughts and feelings to others and to be able to connect with them in meaningful ways. His creativity, playfulness and love of life often made him a handful to watch over. No doubt he could get into more mischief than most kids his age, but he was never a problem for his parents. He learned the household rules easily and most of the time would abide by them.

What happens to these wonderful qualities of curiosity, playfulness, creativity, and an eagerness to learn when children go to school? These traits are suppressed and after a few years all but disappear; all because we try and make children all be the same, to stay in their seats, to color within the lines, to be ready to read by first grade and so on as they progress through the school years. And if they are not ready or do not behave as we expect, then there seems to be a need to label them, to look for what might be wrong with them.

No doubt Kevin can be a handful. Temperamentally these so called "high reactors" are interested more in their environment, and may need more assistance from their primary caregivers and their teachers to settle down. Often times these children are said to have "difficult" temperaments, but should not be labeled as disordered. These children are simply within a wide band of the normal range and showing their unique colors! But might these characteristics also be considered an advantage? I think the answer to this question is a resounding YES, as long as we do not try and label these kids as having problems. In fact I would like to rename this temperamental category to "*Highly Involved*" children.

Kevin's parents had observed his classroom on several occasions and knew their son well. They decided to enroll him in a nearby private school, in hopes that he would experience a better "fit." Since changing schools Kevin is doing very well. He enjoys school, feels safe, is more challenged academically, and is allowed to move around when necessary. There has been no question of ADHD or any other problems at his new school!

Certainly, the smaller number of children in the classroom helps, but that is not the only factor. The current school is described as more flexible and school personnel deal with problems immediately, taking the time to teach each child to respect one another. Differences are seen as strengths, not as weaknesses. Kevin is allowed to be himself and is accepted as a productive and valued member of his community.

Now let's look at the other side of the coin. A diagnosis or a label can have benefits since it can allow a child access to programs and receive professional expertise not otherwise available. Certainly if a child is having difficulty because of a primary neurological or psychological disability it can be helpful to have the correct assessment so the most appropriate treatment can then be obtained.

However, it is not as simple with learning disabilities or other diagnostic categories used in the schools as it might be if the child were diagnosed with strep throat and could then be prescribed the needed antibiotic. Diagnosis of learning disabilities, attention deficit disorder, autism, mental retardation or any other diagnoses schools must deal with are quite different. First of all, these diagnoses do not go away with time. Once diagnosed the labels stick with the children throughout their school years and beyond. The children become the diagnoses.

Teachers often begin to expect less of these children because of their so called disability. Even more sadly, parents may start to look at the child differently and the child's opinion of him/herself changes to one who needs help, or who is different, or inadequate in some essential way, clearly damaging his/her identity. The label lasts a lifetime and these kids are being shortchanged from becoming who they were meant to be . . . all because of a label based upon someone's assessment, which oftentimes is incorrect!

Furthermore, the label in education does not determine the appropriate approach, program or intervention to use with the child! There are numerous treatments or approaches to use with children diagnosed with any of the disorders in which schools must intervene. No one method is the best for learning disabilities, autism, mental retardation or any other label put on a child. Each child must be assisted individually to find the way he/she learns best, which can all be done without labeling the child. Indeed, this is how all children should be taught!

Additionally, educational interventions should be available for all children. We should not make it necessary for a child to be labeled in order to get the services he needs. All children should have access to whatever helps them learn more efficiently, more enthusiastically. Moreover, teachers who are often only minimally trained in what these labels mean, place much too much power and value in these diagnoses. I remember one educator exclaiming her horror when she discovered a child had a very treatable psychological condition. She really saw this child differently; she pitied him and could only see the disorder . . . she lost sight of the child himself. It's different with these disorders because they are not well understood, and because kids don't grow out of them. If a child was physically ill, no one would say that the child was a pneumoniac or a fluic, but if child is autistic, that seems to be all that people see.

When people begin to see the child differently, they then begin to treat the child differently. The child learns to act as if he is helpless and indeed becomes the diagnosis. This is very sad indeed. All the potential that was there at birth, all the other parts of the child that are so normal go unrecognized. The child becomes the disorder. It can be used as a crutch too, used as an excuse to not be able to do more.

Diagnosis does not belong in the schools. Leave it up to the medical professionals, the psychiatrists, and the psychologists who have training to keep the diagnosis in perspective. And parents should be advised to always get a second, independent professional opinion. Undoubtedly, teachers need to know how to teach the child . . . but this can be accomplished without labeling and by opening up services to all children, not just those with labels!

Pessimism is the core result of labeling and diagnosis in our schools. Implied in any diagnosis/label is the unspoken message that there is something wrong with the child, that the child is less capable, that his/her future is potentially changed as a result of this label. Now any psychologist would say this is a misunderstanding and I agree that it is. But nevertheless, effects of labeling tend to change the expectations of the parents, the teachers and the child him/herself. And, the explanation for the child who is not learning is explained by the label . . . rather than by the educational system failing the child!

Certainly, many educational lawyers like the labels; they make their jobs more black and white. But we are doing a dangerous disservice to these children. Labeling or diagnosing is attempting to put the child into a category; and this is not as straightforward as it might appear, because of each individual's uniqueness. Undoubtedly there is a desire to have a neat, organized "cookbook" approach to figuring out why a child is not learning, but it is not a clear cut problem and it is not always because of weaknesses with in the child. Labeling the child keeps us from looking beyond individual weaknesses. It inhibits the discovery of problems within the schools, problems which are interfering with the child's learning. If we start to talk of each child's strengths and needs instead of what is wrong with him/her we'll be on a much better track.

We seem to be on a craze of more intense labeling, just as we are caught up in the testing craze. Both can be quite harmful to our children; both are hidden dangers within our schools. Recently we have seen an increase in the number of children being diagnosed with numerous disorders. Some of this increase in diagnosis may reflect an improved ability to diagnose certain disorders. I believe this is the situation with many of the disorders such as meningitis, encephalitis, whooping cough, and various flus. But I think much more is involved when we see a sudden jump in the diagnoses of ADHD, Autism, Asperger's disorder, and learning disabilities.

Yes, clinicians are becoming more aware and an accurate diagnosis can be helpful to get the child early intervention, when indeed there is a problem. However, autism and other pervasive development disorders are not well defined and too many children seem to fall under these umbrella terms. Children who are often quite unique are placed in such categories, just because they are misunderstood. Frequently the educational interventions would not be different for these children as long as they are learning and receiving assistance to help them acquire social skills and the ability to read social cues. They do not need this label in the schools! Uniqueness should be valued, not treated as a problem.

Let us take a closer look at the characteristics of Asperger's. First of all it is important to understand that until relatively recently people who are currently diagnosed with Asperger's disorder were not classified as having any disorder. They may have been seen as a bit eccentric, possibly as a genius, absented minded in nature and somewhat socially, and possibly physically awkward. Many children may become extremely interested in a subject (which children don't at some time in their lives: dinosaurs, horses, computer games, etc.), which may at times lead the individual to be come extremely successful in a related career later in life.

The most commonly used diagnostic nosologies are the DSM-IV-TR, Diagnostic and Statistical Manual of Mental Disorders (APA, 2000) and the ICD-10, International Classification of Behavioral and Mental Disorders (WHO, 1992). Both are medical texts. To summarize the perspective of these texts, both view Asperger's disorder as a form of autism, although these individuals usually function at a higher level. It's a condition that affects the way a person communicates and relates to others. A number of traits of autism are common to Asperger's disorder including difficulty in social relationships, difficulty in communicating, and limitations in imagination and creative play. There are many diagnosticians that try to break this category down even further into subgroups such as High Functioning Asperger's, Non-verbal LD, etc . . . just more and more labels. What it comes down to is that we all could have some sort of label, but what good would it do us? Indeed it could do us much more harm than good.

There are many well known people who are alleged to have Asperger's although formal diagnoses have not been made. I'll report them here only so that you might to begin to question the need for labels and what might have happened had schools labeled and tried to teach these children to learn in more tradition ways. The list includes Mozart, Albert Einstein, Carl Jung and Sir Isaac Newton! There are also modern-day inventors, businessmen, musicians, politicians and leaders from all walk of life that may fit the diagnostic criteria for AS (Asperger's Resource). Now if, indeed these individuals have had AS it was a gift, not a shortcoming. Why on earth are we bothering to label them? Really what we should be doing is celebrating their uniqueness, their special qualities and fabulous contributions to society and trying to learn from their unique way of seeing and understanding the world. Clearly, medical researchers are making great strides in understanding autism spectrum disorders. Such research is essential and may help identify causal factors and assist with prevention and treatment approaches. My point here is to illustrate that in some cases our differences are our gifts. Those individuals accurately diagnosed with such disorders may well benefit from interventions.

These are not disordered individuals. To try to "fix" these people is to shortchange their potential. We might be missing out on numerous discoveries, inventions, and the gift of diversity. We do not want to limit individuals or inhibit their growth with a harmful label! Instead we want to learn to teach each individual so he/she can learn optimally, and at the same time we might just learn something ourselves.

> If a child can't learn the way we teach, maybe we should learn to teach the way they learn.
>
> —Ignacio Estrada

Chapter 7

Gender Problems that Affect Your Child's Learning

> We are losing young boys to a sense of failure that comes from schooling poorly adapted to their needs. We are losing adolescent males to the depression that comes from feeling neither needed nor respected.
>
> — Joe Manthey, "The Boy Project"

Looking back at our not too distant past I find it amazing it was believed girls were incapable of learning math or science at an advanced level. Girls were expected to learn the basics they would need to balance a checkbook, make change at the grocery store, and understand basic measurements so they could handle cookbook recipes. Well, we've come a long way since those days. However, in many ways we are doing the same thing to our boys today!

Let's take a closer look at Kevin, the adolescent that we met in the preceding chapters. As you remember, Kevin is a thirteen-year-old of at least high average intellectual ability, yet his grades do not reflect his academic gifts. He reports he wants to do well in school, but often does not complete assignments, study for exams, or even ask for help when needed. We now know that he is not ADHD or learning disabled. So what is the problem with Kevin?

Could Kevin be one of those fairly typical adolescent males who do not know how to respond in a setting that unintentionally reinforces the positive academic behavior of females? It seems the male academic needs are not well understood and often overlooked in our schools. In the case of Kevin I believe the issues are far more complex, and run deeper into the very crux of our educational system and our society.

Taking a closer look at overall current statistics and trends in our schools can alert us to some of the problems. It seems girls currently make up 57 percent of college undergraduate students in the United States and females obtain

58 percent of all master's degrees awarded in this country. Furthermore, girls are far outperforming boys in the K-12 academic system. Of those children coded with special needs 70 percent are boys. Beginning at the kindergarten level, boys are expected to achieve a standard that favors girls. Girls used to perform less well than boys on standardized tests until the curriculum was changed to meet the needs of girls (Conlin, 2003). Currently, boys are at a disadvantage with a curriculum that caters to girls, and also on standardized tests which are developed around the curriculum, and so are strongly language-oriented. (Girls tend to excel at earlier ages with language based approaches.) Clearly, we can see that there are gender issues that need to be addressed! The causes of these gender discrepancies appear to be multi-faceted and involve society's perceptions of boys, educational expectations, new state and federal testing policies, school climate, psychological/emotional differences, and brain based and biological differences. Let's take a closer look at each one of these areas.

Society's perceptions and resulting impact on the gender gap involve confining stereotypes which are unfortunately strongly a part of our culture/social norms. For example: girls have an unwritten code which demands that they be thin, pretty, and caregivers while boys are encouraged to be strong, brave, silent, and macho. William Pollack (1998) talks about the "Boy Code," which he describes as an established structure of beliefs regarding how real boys are expected to behave. Unfortunately, these anticipated behaviors often clash with expectations in the classroom. These unwritten rules expect boys to act strong and hide their emotions; it's not acceptable for boys to appear vulnerable in any way. As a result, boys are less likely to speak up in the classroom when having difficulty or frustrated; instead they are more likely to act out or to keep quiet. So, is it possible that Kevin does not ask for help because he might look less masculine? The answer is a resounding YES! Furthermore, this unwritten set of laws is, regrettably, unintentionally and unconsciously reinforced by parents, teachers, coaches, peers and the media! One can easily see that these societal ideals are disruptive to the lives of both boys and girls. However, it is the male code which appears to have the most negative impact on boys' academic performance.

Problems experienced by males are deeply ingrained within our society's belief system. To get a clearer picture of just how profound these beliefs are all you need do is take a trip to the toy store. Walk down the aisles of the store and you will immediately be able to tell which aisles are for boys and which are for girls. Most of the toys which are clearly marketed for boys are those with a dark and violent side. These toys reflect and add force to the boy code, as well as sadly reinforcing our society's problem of increased violence! Might this play into much of the school violence we are seeing? I think the answer is very likely yes!

The "Boy Code" also is implied in many of our common statements we all have heard, or maybe even said, without really understanding the impact it might have on our male children. Such comments as: "Don't throw like a girl," "Don't walk like a girl," "Be strong, don't cry," or "Don't be a sissy," all clearly are meant to make our boys act in a certain manner. Unfortunately, this traps our boys in a web from which it is very difficult to escape and undermines their self-concept.

Additionally, family interactions have a strong influence on male children. As boys mature the closeness between family members, particularly mothers and sons, is often seen as forbidden. This physical separation starts very early for boys and is often forced at a time when the child needs emotional and physical closeness, particularly from his parents. A good example of this is seen when boys first venture out into the world to attend preschool. They are expected to leave without a fuss and be brave little men, while girls are allowed much more freedom to express their fears and their feelings.

When the boys hit adolescence they again are faced with yet another unspoken strained separation increasing the distance from family members at a crucial time in their lives when they need guidance, support, and healthy affection from their parents. William Pollack (1998) believes these early separations are a source of depression in many young males. Depression definitely impacts academic performance.

Emotionally, boys are most clearly at risk in the schools because of these unspoken societal beliefs, but also because of educational expectations, policies, and in many cases detrimental school climates. Boys are really caught in a catch-22. Case in point, we are less tolerant of boys and expect them to act like little men, to be strong and macho. However, we also expect boys to act the same as girls when it comes to academics: to sit still, color inside the lines, have neat hand writing, work cooperatively, be neat and organized, learn in the same sequence and manner (verbal approach rather than experiential) as girls, and demonstrate learning through a standardized testing format which often favor girls as well! Without a doubt the emotional climate in many schools and classrooms favors girls over boys (Connell & Gunzelmann, 2004).

What's more, schools are hurrying children to grow up rapidly and to learn concepts at younger and younger ages. There is a strong downward spiraling of the curriculum and a focus on accountability which has contributed to our current testing obsession. Dr. David Elkind believes that our current testing craze is in part due to the dynamics of our hurrying schools. Indeed, boys may be at a unique disadvantage with standardized testing. Although some boys are able to excel in this manner, this approach is far more beneficial to most girls.

A one-size-fits-all approach to testing is not meeting the needs of all of our children. This movement results in no greater knowledge, but puts additional stress on our children. Additionally, introducing concepts in earlier grades may put boys at greater risk for failure. Many boys are just not ready to learn many of these concepts since many of the necessary skills develop later in boys than in girls. Although boys may be ready to handle certain concepts earlier, these are not usually a part of their early academic curriculum. Actually, the hurrying of the academic curriculum may put both boys and girls in danger of academic problems when content is introduced before a solid foundation is established and before children are cognitively able to comprehend the concepts involved.

All the issues of gender differences, both male and female, could be addressed if we keep in mind the work of Brazelton and Greenspan (2000) who believe that in order for children to learn and thrive we must meet their individual needs. Most schools only give lip service to addressing the needs of all children. In fact, individual educational plans are only used for children who are coded with disabilities. Shouldn't the needs of all children be met? All children develop at different rates, each at his/her own pace. It appears that we are not yet fully addressing the needs of all individuals and our boys are definitely paying a high price.

Each and every one of these concerns lead to many boys being misunderstood and even misdiagnosed with Attention Deficit Disorder, Learning Disability, Oppositional Defiant Disorder, and Conduct Disorder when in fact some are just frustrated, poorly taught children! We know from years of research that many more boys are diagnosed with these disorders than girls!

The psychological harm that results from being misunderstood may be significant for boys and include lowered self-esteem, depression, anxiety, and motivational problems. An alarming trend we are seeing in our country is that younger children are being diagnosed with depression more frequently. Yet we need to be aware that when boys become depressed their symptoms may be ignored or misinterpreted because boys who become depressed tend to be externalizers: they are seen as more antagonistic, aggressive, antisocial, self-indulgent and deceitful (Wenar & Kerig, 2000, p. 147). Therefore, boys may be misunderstood and labeled with oppositional defiant disorder or conduct disorder. They also may have a decreased attention span and an increased activity level as a result of depression, rather than ADHD. Depression in children and specifically in male children does not always look like what is seen in a depressed adult.

Boys' symptoms of psychological distress may present differently too with learning disabilities and with ADHD. There is a wealth of research documenting the large discrepancy between the male-to-female ratio with ADHD (Cited in Biederman, Mick, Faraone, Braaten, Doyle, Spencer, Wilens, Frazier, and Johnson, 2002). And there is comorbidity of ADD with Conduct, Depressive, Anxiety, learning, substance abuse, and other disorders (Biederman, Newcorn, Sprich, 1991). Such constant misunderstanding and awkwardness of fit with one's academic endeavors may lead to a self-defeating downward spiral of issues resulting in lowered academic performance.

There are also biologically-based differences in boys' and girls' brains. Human brains consist of two hemispheres that are intricately connected; however, they process information differently (Baron-Cohen, 2003; Springer and Deutsch, 1998). The left hemisphere processes information analytically and sequentially which allows this hemisphere to focus on details. The left hemisphere also usually has primary responsibility for processing auditory and verbal information. The left brain specializes in comprehending words, and is actively involved in listening, speaking, and writing. In contrast, the processing style of the right hemisphere is intuitive and holistic; it sees the whole picture. The right hemisphere is usually where visual-spatial and visual-motor information is processed. Our right brain specializes in visual-spatial-motor activities such as sports, architecture, sculpture, painting, and carpentry (Connell, 2002).

So, while boys and girls begin kindergarten and first grade at the same ages they have different developmental strengths and weaknesses. Girls' left hemispheres are more developed than those of boys (Gurian, 2001). In essence, brain biology permits girls to read and write using the "traditional approaches" at a younger age. In contrast, according to Gurian (2001), boys' right hemispheres are more developed, allowing them to learn easier using non-traditional approaches involving movement and utilizing visual spatial skills. These brain based differences have been documented in the research using norm-referenced intelligence and achievement measures. Vogel (2001) writes:

> In general fextor the normally achieving population, a substantial body of research confirms the higher verbal ability of females including global verbal abilities as measured by the WISC Verbal subtests, grammar, word fluency, and spelling and higher visual-spatial and mathematical abilities of males. (p. 50)

Conventionally, teachers have encouraged boys to learn to read and write in a traditional manner, understanding that developmentally boys would catch up around the 4th grade. Our country's current focus on high-stakes state and federal tests generally works in favor of the brain strengths of girls, and against those of boys, especially at the lower grade levels. Achievement data from No Child Left Behind (NCLB) showed that in all fifty states, boys are behind girls in reading and math. However, these test scores do not give an accurate picture of boys' abilities. For example, boys can learn their letters by first making the letters out of clay; they can act out the punctuation marks; and they can read by incorporating phonics using technology.

Although boys used to catch up with the girls around 4th grade, this is no longer the case. Today, with the pressure of the state and federal tests experienced by teachers and students alike, boys are feeling pressure and stress that is harmful to them. Instead of catching up, they are giving up! School is often seen by boys as "a girl thing." (Connell & Gunzelmann, 2004)

So, what can we do to improve this dreadful academic situation for boys? Clearly, there are psychological and biological differences between boys and girls which result in differences in the way society perceives boys, how parents and the schools interact with male students, and in the resulting emotional responses of boys. For the past thirty years our girls have been supported by the influential Women's Movement. In 1972, Congress passed Title IX that provided gender equity in schools across America. Today, there is increased awareness of professors, teachers, and parents across America who encourage girls to take advanced courses, participate in sports, and to do their best work. Clearly, we need to continue to support our girls; however, at the same time we must also begin to focus on ways to help our boys. It's time to address the individual needs of all children!

There are numerous things we can do to help all children succeed academically. First and foremost we can create positive and supportive home and school environments for all children by challenging the Boy Code and the unwritten Girl Code. We all need to confront our beliefs about how boys and girls should look and behave. Boys can be genuine boys and not be caught in a catch-22 if we encourage them to express their feelings and to be true to themselves. They should not be forced into false roles to "fit in." Girls should be encouraged to accept themselves for who they are . . . they do not need to fit some ideal "Barbie Doll " image or live up to a superwoman's standard. They also can be quite feminine and successful! Strong, healthy male and female role models are needed in our schools: models who are not buying into these unhealthy codes (Gunzelmann & Connell, 2005).

We also can change curriculum and the teaching approaches when needed! Why not introduce concepts to boys on their timetable? Allowing for individual and gender differences is essential. Many boys are not ready to sit still and color between the lines at young ages. They should not be made to feel inferior by receiving lower grades, being reprimanded, or medicated because they develop at different rates than girls. We don't need to change the boys, but we definitely need to change the methods including the assessment approaches!

In closing, as parents we have our work cut out for us—we must keep the girls soaring, while at the same time opening the cage and letting the boys fly too. The key is to understand that the boys' flight patterns are different from the girls; we must acknowledge and encourage both.

Many boys think that their grade schools are boy-unfriendly. I well remember my son bursting into the kitchen one day after school, yelling 'They want us to be girls, Mom, they want us to be girls!"

—P. Dalton, "When Did We Lose Sight of Boys?"
(*Washington Post,* Sunday, May 9, 1999)

Chapter 8

Paradoxical Safety Problems that Affect Student Learning

"Listen to your children." They will tell you, perhaps not directly but by their behavior, whether they feel safe at school. They may often want to stay in bed in the morning, or they'll have mysterious stomachaches, or they'll have lots of unexplained absences. Those are "illnesses" that a visit to the doctor cannot cure, but a visit to the school might.

—(John Merrow, 2004)

Safety in the schools involves much more than metal detectors and disaster plans. Although such catastrophe planning is necessary, we are overlooking some less obvious issues that put our children's everyday safety and education at risk. It appears that some of our current practices designed to ensure student safety are actually increasing safety concerns. As we learned in chapter 3 from Drs. Brazelton and Greenspan (2000), all children require physical protection, safety, and regulation in order to grow, learn, and flourish. The obvious safety issues are clear-cut and usually well addressed in our schools. However, there are less obvious, paradoxical *hidden dangers* in our schools that impact the social, cognitive and emotional well being of our students.

These hidden dangers are not always immediately apparent, or may be taken for granted as being helpful and therefore are not identified as problematic. However, I believe these risks are contributing to a crisis which includes more school violence, more behavioral and emotional problems, more students unable to attain basic skills, and students now feeling unsafe.

Chapter 8

PARADOXICAL REACTIONS TO SAFETY POLICIES

Since the Columbine shootings and September 11, we have seen a dramatic increase in cases of Post Traumatic Stress Disorder and other anxiety disorders, as well as an increase in cases of depression. Given that the issues in our schools often reflect the larger issues seen in our society, it is not surprising that there is an increase in anxiety disorders and depression among our schooled-aged children. I suspect that this increase is in part due to the overreaction of many adults, in an attempt to protect our children, which may unintentionally be increasing our children's stress levels and paradoxically making our schools less safe than before. School lock downs, armed police in the schools, metal detectors, crisis response teams, surveillance cameras, and other high-tech law enforcement personnel procedures and equipment are now quite common in our school buildings. In fact schools are becoming increasingly similar to jails and juvenile detention centers; certainly not a climate conducive to enhanced academic learning.

Clearly, we all have much to learn from the work of our law enforcement agencies, and their services are vital to our society. One very enlightening document published regarding school violence was researched as a joint endeavor by the United States Secret Service and the United States Department of Education, titled: *The Final Report and Findings of the Safe School Initiative: Implications for the Prevention of School Attacks in the United States.* Undoubtedly, this document is a reflection of our society over the past many years and there is a considerable amount of well conducted research and information generated from this effort. Nonetheless, when one reads this document and looks at how this information has been interpreted and applied in our schools it is obvious that we really need to make some adjustments. I am in no way criticizing this important document; merely trying to look at what else might be needed, and assess the fallout from faulty attempts to make our schools safer places.

I was initially surprised to see the U.S. Secret Service working with the U.S. Department of Education, but the benefit of these agencies combining their expertise soon became apparent to me. However, what also became clearer as I read the report was the mind-set in the interpretation of data obtained from previous school violence incidents: it was interpreted primarily from a martial and law enforcement perspective. What was glaringly left out of this report was the vast amount of accumulated knowledge from educators, psychologists, sociologists, pediatricians, and other professionals with child development expertise. There needs to be much more collaboration in conducting the research, interpreting the results, and most particularly in the implementation of the findings!

We are truly out of balance in our schools when we do not approach educating our children with an evenhanded perspective gleaned from all experts in related fields. Instead, the balance has shifted toward an adult reactionary need to anticipate, plan, and control every conceivable catastrophe. This makes all of us more wary, uneasy and anxious; yet really no safer. It is irrational to believe we can plan for every possibility that may happen, and we should not be worrying our children about every possible tragedy that could intrude upon their lives. It can be equated with having drills in the schools for how one should react if a meteor hit the building; the likelihood of this occurrence is slight. In the event that it did happen, then the adults in charge would call in whatever emergency services were needed. Certainly our military, police, firemen, and emergency medical teams need to have very specific training in order to deal with crises, and the general public should be advised of planned procedures, but our children should not have to worry and be literally overwhelmed by the changing world in which we are living.

Regrettably, children are learning the world is not safe, but unfortunately they are also learning their schools are not safe places either. All children need do to confirm these ideas is to look around on any given day to observe metal detectors, armed police, lock downs drills, and various other disaster planning maneuvers played out in their classrooms. These so-called safety measures are sometimes acted out in full riot gear requiring the children to put cardboard over the windows, and to remain silent and hide under their desks. Teachers are required to do the same. If a child is left out in the hallway or has been to the bathroom, he/she no longer has access to the hypothetical safety zone within the classroom!

The professionals in charge here really need to stop and ask the question: "What are we thinking here?" To a young child these drills are nothing short of terrifying—with police charging around, with guns and their parents not allowed into the buildings. Young children are being emotionally harmed by these drills which are occurring in most schools across the country. What we are doing is teaching our children to be fearful, that their neighborhood is a very dangerous place to be. It's not to say the world isn't a more dangerous place today; certainly it is, but we can help our children to know basic safety behaviors without causing permanent harm to their fundamental sense of trust.

Have we all forgotten the well known psycho-social theory of Erik Erikson? The first and very critical stage is for children to be able to develop a basic sense of trust before we are able to move onto higher stages. Most parents do an exemplary job helping their infants learn to trust them during their early years. This critical foundation of trust is essential to negotiating higher stages, and current practices are eroding this essential base.

Psychologists, educators and other child development specialists also are aware of Abraham Maslow's work on human motivation and the implications on learning. Maslow's theory clearly depicts the indispensable need for safety near the base of the hierarchy, well before one can feel a sense of belonging and self-esteem, and then only to begin learning the tasks at hand. (Readers wanting a more in-depth description of Maslow's or Erickson's theories are directed to read their original works or a summary in Schultz and Schultz, 2001)

We also must consider the cognitive developmental levels of the children. Jean Piaget's widely researched and replicated studies clearly show that children do not think in the same manner as most adults. Children, particularly pre-teens, are not able to think in "what if" terms. They may see in these practice drills that the real event is likely to happen. The younger the child the more vulnerable he/she is to this harmful misunderstanding, and the less able he/she is to comprehend there isn't a terrorist actually standing right around the corner, or lurking in the next classroom.

Indeed we will see more issues of anxiety, hopelessness, and difficulties learning. Even more concerning are those malleable young minds that get caught up in the excitement and the intensity of the drama and beginning to identify with the need to fight violence with violence. Albert Bandura's Social Learning Theory clearly demonstrates how children copy their models. Children may well not be able to learn their academic subjects as well under such highly stressful times, but you can be sure they will be learning from the models of force parading around the schools. And are we drawing so much attention to these issues through the news, media and by our over responses that schools may indeed be inadvertently encouraging copycat behavior, and inadvertently reinforcing more school violence? This is a very dangerous practice indeed. (If more information is needed on Bandura's theory the reader is directed to Schultz & Schultz, 2001.)

We also are truly out of balance in our schools when we take into account the martial mentality in our schools. It may make many adults feel more in control to be doing something in the name of safety, but it really is an illusion. There really is a hidden curriculum demanding obedience and conformity in many of our schools (Mosca & Hollister, 2004; Saltman & Gabbard, 2003). Furthermore, Giroux believes that young people are quickly realizing that schools have more in common with military boot camps and prisons than they do with other institutions in American society (2003, p. 562).

Let's take for example the zero tolerance policies that many schools now have in place. A zero tolerance policy has no open-mindedness for any wrongdoing no matter how inconsequential or understandable a situation may be. We need to question our need for such extreme policies. Upon first hearing of such policies parents may believe that zero tolerance could help to make a school a safer place to be. But like so many other plans in life, what might look good on paper, plays out quite differently in real life. We also must ask ourselves why we think such drastic measures are a current need. Are most of our children so out of control that they don't know right from wrong? The Reverend Jesse Jackson believes that: *"Fear of our children is at the heart of zero tolerance policies in our schools"* (cited in Mosca & Hollister, 2004; Ayers, Dohrn, & Ayers, 2001). I think he may be right. Zero tolerance is reinforcing the belief that children cannot be trusted.

Many schools have adopted zero tolerance policies particularly concerning weapons, drugs and alcohol. At first glance these policies may appear to make sense and to protect our children; but in actuality they can be quite detrimental and even at times may increase the risk to children. According to Farberman (2006) the American Psychological Association's Zero Tolerance Task Force reviewed research on the effects of zero tolerance policies over a ten year period. The task force determined "that such policies not only fail to make schools safe or more effective in handling student behavior, they actually increase the instances of problem behavior and dropout rates" (p. 27).

There are numerous extreme zero tolerance cases that can be cited to depict the problems inherent in these policies. Let's take for example the case of an adolescent male who used mouthwash on school premises. Since the mouthwash contained alcohol, he was harshly punished, with the police being called in. This young man did not drink the mouthwash; he merely used it to freshen his breath which is an age-appropriate behavior for self-conscious adolescents (Zero Tolerance Nightmare Stories, 2003).

There are also numerous well documented cases of harsh and unreasonable consequences resulting from zero tolerance policies. Included in these cases are incidents involving the writing of a scary Halloween story as a class assignment, stealing $2.00 from another student, and the vague threat by a 12-year-old student that he was "going to get" students if they ate all the potatoes in the school lunch line. Unbelievably, this child spent two weeks in jail! (ABA, 2000; see also Koch, 2000; Black, 2004 for cases and alarming statistics.)

In so many cases it appears the zero tolerance policies trump reason. In the above reported cases the authorities were called in, no one listened to the individual circumstances involved. In numerous cases responsible young people have faced legal procedures, and potential youth imprisonment to the horror of their parents and I'm sure to their friends as well. These unfortunate situations have resulted in needless legal cases, undue hardship for parents and regrettably an extreme distrust toward the schools and various authority figures.

Another important finding is that zero tolerance policies unfairly target minority and disadvantaged youth. One of the most infamous cases occurred in Decatur, Illinois where seven students were expelled for a two-year period after a brawl at a high school football game. Jesse Jackson believed that the harsh disciplinary action was racially biased and was instrumental in having the ruling reduced (MacNeil-Lehrer Newshour, 1999). It appears that there are alarming statistics depicting that zero tolerance policies appear to unfairly discriminate as reported by the American Educational Research Association (2000) and a 2001 report from Harvard University's Civil Rights Project, titled "Zero Tolerance: Unfair, with Little Recourse" (Cited in Black, 2004).

It appears students who are learning disabled were also over represented as offenders of zero tolerance policies.(Civil Rights Project Harvard University, 2003). Students from lower socioeconomic levels with fewer alternatives are also likely to be over represented in this offending group. Obviously, zero tolerance policies are not conducive to safe school environments. Instead zero tolerance policies may be establishing dangerous school climates.

So just what are our children learning from such extreme measures? They are learning not to tell people in authority when they suspect that someone might have a dangerous weapon or may potentially be threatening another. To the children, particularly to adolescents, the adults in authority clearly do not listen and overreact to the slightest situations. They do not want to get their friends in trouble over a potentially small incident. Unfortunately, when there may be a serious threat, students may not speak up! They also do not want to be put in the position of being a nark or a tattle tale; a compromising social situation for any child.

Furthermore, harassment, threats and intimidation of students takes place routinely when zero tolerance policy are in effect. This only increases our teens' distrust and alienation from adults, or increases their own anxieties about being in a school's climate that clearly does not trust or respect the students! This brat camp mentality establishes schools that are not places of learning, but places where control is paramount and differences are seen as threats. These are schools that break the spirit of our youth. Children become hopeless, anxious, depressed, and pessimistic, alienated from their true selves. These are very toxic climates indeed.

The Zero Tolerance Policies go against all that we know we should do in the schools: take each case on an individualized basis, listen to the child, and understand the whole situation. Even the American Bar Association (2000) voted against mandatory zero tolerance policies in the schools; still, more and more schools are adopting these regulations.

"Fear and reactionary politics, rather than sound reasoning, have driven the zero tolerance movement and led, in fact, to schools that are less safe" (Mosca & Hollister, 2004).

SOCIAL HARMS: BULLIES & CLIQUES

There are other red-flag issues pertaining to our children's safety that we must become more aware of too. One of the biggest problems in our schools involves bullying. School administrators are well aware that this occurs and spend a great deal of time and energy developing anti-bullying policies. So often anti-bullying programs and policies look good on paper but are ineffective or even ignored by students and some school personnel!

Bullying is a widespread phenomenon that involves tormenting victims through various means including all types of harassment, assault, or attempts to manipulate or coerce victims. It can take several destructive forms including verbal, physical, sexual, racial, and emotional. One of the more recent developments involves cyber bullying which occurs through emails, instant messaging, cell phones, text messaging and other technological approaches. Cyber bullying can be severely harmful reaching the victim even in the shelter of his/her home and also spreads the vicious messages to untold numbers across the internet almost instantaneously.

Children who are bullied suffer from anxiety, depression and lowered self-esteem. Bullying interferes with learning as well. Over time children who are bullied repeatedly may retreat and feel hopeless, or they may become angry and act out. Oftentimes children who are the bullies engage in more anti-social acts. Emotional bullying can be more subtle, but no less damaging. School lunchrooms are notorious for this type of bullying where students are avoided or not allowed to sit at certain tables. This type of abuse or bullying occurs frequently due to cliques. Cliques are destructive and should not be confused with groups of friends. It's healthy to have a strong peer group with similar interests, but cliques involve a strict code of membership and behaviors in order to belong. The purpose of a clique is for status and popularity where a friendship involves shared values and beliefs (Kids Health, 2005). Girls tend to engage in verbal, emotional and cyber-bullying, where boys more often get involved with the physical types. Both genders can be quite cruel, particularly beginning in middle school grades when they may not realize the extent of harm and pain they are causing their classmates. Racial slurs and sexual innuendo are particularly damaging to the developing sense of self.

Another serious concern is that school personnel, at times, engage in bullying and harassing the students too! "Children are quietly tormented in ways that adults in charge appear to either willfully ignore or silently approve" (Meier, 2004, p. 58). On numerous occasions I have heard of teachers using intimidation tactics to get a student to behave in a desired manner. Calling a students a name, even when it is meant in jest, is even more harmful when coming from an adult in authority. Names such as

"Space Cadet," "Hyper" or "Lazy" imply a damaging label which can have long term harmful implications. Names like "Idiot," "Jerk" and "Stupid" have no business on the lips of teachers either, but have been reported by teacher-bullied students on numerous occasions. I realize children, particularly adolescents, can push adults to say things they do not mean. However, if this happens the adults must be aware of the damaging effects of their statements and make amends.

School personnel at times ignore or gloss over bullying when they see it in the schools. For example one student described a scene in a seventh grade classroom that occurred when a couple from the popular clique made derogatory remarks to a girl about her appearance and her clumsy behavior. The teacher's response was to quietly laugh; which encourages this type of bullying to continue. This young girl has reportedly been bullied since she began school in kindergarten. Why would a teacher do such a thing one might ask? Well, I'm not sure the teacher was even aware of his behavior. This was not an intentionally mean adult; I suspect that he unconsciously did not want to confront the popular clique and lose face in their eyes. You see, he was seen as one of the "cool teachers." Teachers have their cliques too!

Then there is the case of Luke. Luke is an adolescent who complained that school was contrary to his learning and development. Socially he did not fit in the "cool" cliques and at times, he was bullied by some of the other students. Although school personnel tried to help Luke with "his problem," in some ways the faculty and staff were a part of the problem! Some believed he just needed to "toughen up" while others tried to overprotect him. Both approaches left Luke feeling inadequate and unsafe in his academic environment.

When reviewing statistics on school violence I found that numerous cases involved severe and prolonged bullying. Our schools are not safe when bullying is occurring. Why is this being allowed to happen in our schools? Bullying is not a normal part of childhood behavior. It is learned behavior and has become deeply ingrained in many schools' cultures. But what our children need to learn is to respect, understand and appreciate individual differences and diversity; not to shun or bully classmates for their uniqueness. A quote from J. Noonan (2004) sums up the social ills impacting school safety:

> The development of strong and sustainable relationships will contribute more in the end to a healthy and safe school than metal detectors ever will, and our ability to instruct our students how to develop sustainable relationships of their own is as essential a skill as math and reading. (Noonan, 2004, p. 65)

OUT OF CONTROL CLASSROOMS

However, there are problems contributing to safety issues in the schools and there are times when some children need special placements where they will be accepted, while they are working on their behaviors so they can be included successfully in regular classrooms. In Chapter 3 we were introduced to the case of Sally. Her situation illustrates problems which occur frequently. To refresh your memory, Sally was experiencing symptoms of anxiety and attention problems; not from a deficit of her own, but because of an out-of-control classroom. There were twenty-eight children; two of the children had severe behavioral problems and required a lot of extra time from the teacher who had no education or experience to handle problems of this magnitude.

Teachers cannot handle all the severe issues that are being mainstreamed into their classrooms. Schools have been including children in regular classrooms under the guise that they should be allowed to have the same educational experience as other children. I couldn't agree more, as long as other children are not put at risk of injury or continually deprived of instruction time, and as long as the mainstreamed child is receiving the best educational interventions, not just passing time as so often is the case.

Schools do this to save money! Having too many children in out-of-district placement costs a lot of money. However, if the child receives the appropriate schooling early (without the need for a label and without the needless and excessive costs of educational lawyers) then all children will benefit, and more serious problems will be prevented. Children who are underserviced in the schools, or for whom the school just is not a good "fit," are oftentimes the ones being bullied and developing secondary problems; sometimes with quite serious ramifications as a result!

CURRICULUM CONCERNS

One other serious hidden safety concern which really needs to be revamped involves relatively common curriculum selections. Children are very impressionable; we all know this fact. We also know that it is more difficult to keep children interested in the classroom today than it was 30 and 40 years ago. Today's children are used to technology with all the special effects; they can easily become bored with the curriculum.

In an attempt to make the classroom an interesting place many teachers are resorting to curriculum which is definitely sensation seeking, but may be contributing to problems for our children. I'm referring to programs of study that include the darker side of children's literature where violence and suicide are not uncommon themes; to science lectures that focus more on the "guts and gore" than on understanding the process, and even to history lessons that use Hollywood version movies about wars, all in an attempt to entertain the children. Unfortunately, they are learning lessons teachers never meant to teach and as a result our children are at more risk emotionally. We may be contributing to children's increasing rate of anxiety, depression and even violence.

The well-documented classic research of Albert Bandura (1965) and numerous other current social cognitive theorists partially explains my concerns here. Both humans and animals are capable of vicarious learning or learning by observing others. The models presented in some children's literature, movies, etc. are not necessarily the ones we want our children modeling. Of course not all children will perform such undesirable behaviors. However, under certain circumstances some children will perform them. Even more disturbing is the fact that all the children exposed to such models have learned the behavior whether they act upon it or not! I believe we have a responsibility to make sure our children are exposed to healthy models whenever possible and to *take the time* to help children process and fully understand the situations when they inevitably come across harmful models in the news and their everyday lives.

In précis, parents must be very cognizant of what schools are teaching regarding the safety policies and procedures, and how the schools assist children in overcoming the negative pressures within the culture that encourages cliques and bullying. Furthermore, we must help to develop safer school climates that foster an appreciation for individual differences and diversity. Then our schools will be safer places for our children to thrive.

> It may be that only when we create truly more interesting schools will they be safer places. In short, too much of our discussion of safety misses the real target.
>
> —Meier (2004, p. 55)

Chapter 9

Buildings that Negatively Impact Your Child's Learning

There are also numerous hidden dangers in our school buildings which many parents may assume are being properly handled. After all, schools are public buildings and they house our most precious resources: our children. However, very often this may not be the case. Many of our nation's school facilities are dated with problems such as asbestos and a host of environmental contaminants. Even in newer buildings there are real causes for concern. For example, some new school buildings have been erected on land fills. The land was available and the price was right, but what about the toxic chemicals just below the surface? To think our children are playing on playgrounds that were once dumps! What are officials thinking here?

Let's take a closer look at some of these very real concerns in our schools today. Our country is growing rapidly. According to information from the U.S. Census Bureau, the United States' population reached 281,421,906 in 2000 with current estimates over 299,000,000 (U.S. Census 2000; Population Reference Bureau, 1999). Furthermore, the U.S. Census Bureau predicts our population is rising rapidly and will continue to do so! With statistics like these we undoubtedly have a growth problem and a very real predicament with providing safe and first-rate schools for our nation's children.

It is understandable with the current and projected population growth rates that the Environmental Protection Agency is looking into the feasibility of allowing more schools to be built on brownfields. According to the EPA, "a brownfield site is real property, the expansion, redevelopment, or reuse of which may be complicated by the presence or potential presence of a hazardous substance, pollutant, or contaminant" (U.S. Environmental Protection Agency, 2007b).

The Brownfields Revitalization Act became law in 2002. This law provides financial assistance to eligible applicants and apparently schools are allowed to use such brownfields to build educational facilities once these sites are cleaned up. The land is available and the price is considerably lower than purchasing virgin or other prime real estate. Vague terminology is being used such as "sufficiently decontaminated" when there are no established levels of safety available based upon long-term research. Determining what might be a sufficient level of decontamination is a risky practice since children are much more susceptible to toxins in the environment than are otherwise healthy adults. This is because their nervous and endocrine systems are less developed and much more susceptible to harmful chemical messengers. The younger the child, the more the susceptibility (*Children's Environmental Health Network, 2005*). Therefore, without long-term research on the effects of these supposedly cleaned-up sites I believe we are playing Russian Roulette with the lives of our children. Certainly these sites do need to be cleaned up; but the use of such reclaimed sites should be for sustainable purposes than educating our children. Trying to save a buck yet risking the very futures of our children and ultimately our nation seems to be penny wise and pound foolish!

AIR QUALITY

Air Quality concerns are another major concern in our nation's schools. By reviewing anecdotal information, the news stories and a variety of other sources we can easily detect that a wide range of indoor air problems are occurring. These result in costly, time consuming interventions, including school evacuations and emergency repairs. Astoundingly, in 1996 the U.S. Government Accounting Office released data indicating that over half of our schools have problems which affect indoor air quality!

Many of our nation's schools were built in the 1950's and earlier at times when building codes and related safety concerns were not as compelling. We now know there are significant health related issues related to asbestos, radon, toxic molds, pesticides, numerous cleaning products, and even glues and other toxins used in the building and carpeting of new buildings! Nonetheless, there seems to be a disconnect between health and safety issues, based upon solid research, and the repairing of these building violations and necessary precautions for use of new materials and products.

Many building materials used back even a decade or two ago have been banned including products including asbestos which are in numerous building materials: floor and ceiling tiles, older siding and roofing products, not to mention in some cases in walls, heating elements and insulation. Certainly the mitigation of asbestos from our schools is a costly process, but one that needs to be addressed sooner rather than later. (See U.S. Environmental Protection Agency, 2007a)

Many schools are still in process of making such repairs; others have done so, but may have had shoddy work done. Additionally, regular air quality testing should be done on a routine basis to assure the levels remain at safe levels. Why has it taken so long to address this issue in our schools when the risk of asbestos exposure has been known for many years now? Yet in many instances the general public was not well aware of such concerns.

We know that there is not an established safe level of asbestos, so we need to be more vigilant to make sure our children are exposed to as little as possible. Back in May of 2000 headline news focused on the fact that asbestos had been found in children's crayons (Schneider & Smith, 2000)! Even the Consumer Product Safety Commission (CPSC) was caught off guard by these findings. Apparently the talc used in crayons to make them less waxy may have asbestos mixed in as a result of the mining process. This just goes to show that all products used by children should be regularly monitored for quality standards (Schneider & Smith, 2000; Consumer Product Safety Commission, 2000).

Radon is another serious health concern, not usually addressed in our schools. Radon can have harmful effects in both our drinking water and our air. If the water is from public sources the radon levels are carefully monitored. If water is obtained from private sources, then this may or may not be addressed. We know that repeated, prolonged exposure to radon causes lung cancer in both smokers and nonsmokers (U.S. Environmental Protection Agency, 2007f). Yet, according to the EPA, radon-related examination of 29 schools across the country resulted in poor ventilation being discovered in most of the schools. Also, nearly one in five schools is estimated to have at least one classroom with radon measures above the EPA recommended levels (U.S. Environmental Protection Agency, 2007f; see also U.S. Environmental Protection Agency, 1994).

These are very disturbing findings, no doubt. But the most disturbing information is that radon testing is not routinely conducted in the schools. It is done on only a voluntary basis! Furthermore, if radon is detected, the school may or may not choose to address the problem! The Environmental Protection Agency has no regulatory or enforcement authority regarding general indoor air quality in our nation's schools! This is outrageous! (See U.S. Environmental Protection Agency, 2007e; Santilli, 2002)

Living in a nation where school buildings are aging and where buildings are subjected to the powerful effects of nature—storms, winds, ice, temperature changes—raise the possibilities of cracking, settling and eventually leaking. Leaks bring water damage which frequently results in the buildup of toxic molds.

The case of Carol clearly illustrates the serious consequences of molds in schools buildings. Carol is an only child of an intact professional family. Carol's parents changed their daughter's school during 3rd grade because of chronic health problems. She was allergic to high levels of mold in her school building and was frequently sick from secondary infections. As a result she needed to be on allergy medication which caused her to feel tired and unmotivated. The side effects of the medication and numerous absences from school interfered with her progress academically. Carol's parents consulted with her medical doctors and as a result requested that the school building be tested for molds not routinely considered during air quality assessment. The results came back positive for elevated levels of mold contamination. School administrators wanted to code (label) the child with the problem when in reality it was the building that was unhealthy and unsafe for all of its inhabitants!

Unfortunately, Carol developed multiple antibiotic allergies from frequent and chronic usage of antibiotics due to infections which would not clear while she remained in the polluted school environment. We know the need for extensive use of antibiotics is a risk to all our citizens since bacteria build up resistance to antibiotics at an alarming rate and render them ineffective. This allows for the development of super bugs which do not respond to typical antibiotic treatment.

Medical researchers are discovering that

> In the United States and globally, many other infectious germs, including those that cause pneumonia, ear infections, acne, gonorrhea, urinary tract infections, meningitis, and tuberculosis, can now outwit some of the most commonly used antibiotics and their synthetic counterparts, antimicrobials. According to the Mayo Clinic in Rochester, Minn., drug resistance may have contributed to the 58 percent rise in infectious disease deaths among Americans between 1980 and 1992 (Nordenberg, 1998).

Furthermore, David Bell, M.D., of Centers for Disease Control and Prevention, states that "virtually all important human pathogens treatable with antibiotics have developed some resistance" (Nordenberg, 1998). The U.S. Centers for Disease Control and Prevention believes this resistance to be one the world's most pressing public health problems!

Carol was forced to change schools because she was always sick with secondary infections due to the severity of the pollution and lack of responsiveness to the contamination by school personnel! Once her school environment was changed Carol no longer suffered from chronic secondary sinus infections. Most common colds ran a more typical course, never needing antibiotic interventions, and she found it much easier to focus on her academic studies too! Her case represents only one example of the serious health and safety issues which clearly impact the long-term well-being and academic success of all of our children.

Asthma and allergies have been increasing at alarming rates over the past many years. In 2003 the Center for Disease Control estimated that 19.8 million Americans were suffering from asthma, indicating a serious health problem (Center for Disease Control, 2005). Furthermore, the National Heart, Lung, and Blood Institute (NHLBI) reported asthma symptoms doubling during the previous 15 years (cited in National Institute of Health, 2001). In the United States alone the rates of mortality from asthma, hospitalizations, and emergency room visits have been increasing, especially among children and African American populations. We can no longer afford to ignore these alarming statistics and evidence that indoor pollutants trigger asthma and related problems in our children and school personnel (see National Institute of Environmental Health Services, 2006).

OTHER SCHOOL ENVIRONMENTAL CONCERNS

The well being of a school building is often overlooked as a safety issue, but is a very real concern which affects the learning and health of all of our children. Carol's issues were specific and could clearly be documented. But we need to question the health and safety of our schools in others areas as well . . . areas that may not be as easy to measure except with longitudinal studies.

The manner in which our school buildings are renovated, remodeled or newly built needs to be carefully scrutinized for materials used in building. For example, many schools use carpeting to cover over floor tiles containing asbestos. First of all this is not an adequate intervention for containing the potentially friable asbestos particles, particularly when carpeting needs to be replaced and is torn up disturbing the tiles underneath.

Even in new school buildings where carpeting is often used in the classrooms to cut down on noise level, it brings with it a host of environmental concerns. Predominantly when the synthetic carpeting is new, residual chemicals leach into the environment from the adhesives used and from the synthetic materials in the carpets themselves. Such chemical contaminants can cause a variety of allergies and chemical sensitivities in some individuals impacting health, behavior and learning.

Carpets also hold dust mites, pet dander and other common allergens, increasing the potential for student and teacher allergic and asthmatic reactions. When children spill their milk or other drinks, as all children at times will do, or when buildings leak as they do at times, carpeting is a breeding ground for molds with all the inherent problems discussed above!

This brings us to the toxic chemicals used to clean school buildings, even those used to inhibit the growth of molds! Many chemical cleaners are considered pesticides, with serious potential health risks. Most public schools today have lists of cleaning products which are acceptable when used under specific guidelines. But we should clearly understand that these chemicals are highly noxious, and to many individuals actually disrupt their ability to function in these environments. We probably all can remember returning to school after a vacation to a school with highly cleaned and polished floors! Well, even these polishes used contain potentially harmful ingredients which may cause many people to actually feel nauseous and to have headaches as a result. Clearly these may be our more sensitive individuals; but these chemicals are not good for anyone.

We should also be aware that regular pesticide application is routine for many of our schools to prevent insects, rodents and other undesirable creatures from taking over the buildings. With the use of many of these chemicals we are contaminating the very environment we are trying to protect! The United States Environmental Protection Agency reports that all pesticides are poisonous to some extent (USEPA, 1992).

Even the fertilizers and weed killers used to beautify the school grounds are putting our children at risk. Additionally, we must remember that children are more sensitive than adults to harmful chemicals because of their size and development, and due to the differences in the manner they interact with the environment. Children are much more likely to play on the lawns, play grounds, sports fields or sit on the floor both inside and outside their school buildings. At times some of these chemicals are accidentally ingested through unwashed hands. Pesticides are frequently used in the schools in the cafeterias, kitchens, classrooms, offices, locker rooms, bathrooms, storage rooms, basements and even in day care rooms according to one research report from the New York Schools. Parents and students are often not aware when these applications occur (USEPA, 1992).

Pesticides have a long list of related exposure problems including both acute and long term risks including headache, nausea, dizziness, abdominal cramps, vision problems, persistent weight loss, toxic psychosis, convulsions, skin irritations, vomiting, sensory and behavioral problems, sweating, coughing spasms, reproductive effects, anorexia, ulcers of the mouth and pharynx, and they may be carcinogenic. Clearly all systems in the human body may be affected (USEPA ,1989).

Many of these chemicals are neurotoxins . . . the effects of which may not be seen until many years later. They not only impact the health of our children, but these chemicals can impact their ability to learn as well. Some studies have suggested there is a correlation between the use of lawn chemicals and learning disabilities. Certainly we should not be using any chemicals in our schools or around our children that are even questionable. You may refer to the National Clearinghouse for Educational Resources for lists of acceptable and problematic cleaning products currently used in the schools.

Believe it or not there are still school buildings with lead paint problems too! If a school building was built before 1978, then it probably does contain lead paint. Buildings erected after 1992 probably do not have a lead paint problem. Also, the older the building (usually) the higher the lead paint levels according to the Natural Resources Defense Council. Lead paint is a serious safety hazard for young children, since eating even one paint chip can give a child lead poisoning. Intact lead paint is still a potential problem. Eventually it will deteriorate, and in the meantime it may be releasing lead dust. Removal of intact paint, however, could release higher levels of lead inside the school than leaving the paint in place (Kids Health, 2005). Lead paint in children causes learning difficulties, mental retardation and in some cases even death!

Conclusive evidence is not yet available regarding some of the newer products and technology used in our schools. Even the use of certain lighting in the schools needs to be questioned. Fluorescent and high-density discharge lamps do damage our environment if disposed of improperly due to the mercury content in these lamps. The use of technology may increase our exposure to potentially harmful environmental factors as well. Testing so far is not definitive in these areas, but at least research is ongoing.

Looking back over these chapters it is a wonder we are still able to get up in the mornings and get ourselves out the door! But we cannot be consumed with fear; nor should we just dismiss these issues by saying such trivializing statements as: "Well, this is just the world we live in." No, it doesn't have to be this dangerous, and we need to pay attention to our environment when we are seeing such serious increases in learning and behavioral problems, attention deficit disorders, autism spectrum disorders, anxiety issues, depression, suicide, increased violence, allergies, asthma, childhood obesity and eating disorders, let alone increases in cancer and other serious health problems! The hidden dangers in our schools are putting our nation at risk!

All students have the right to expect a safe and healthy environment . . . The health of our children demands no less.

—Keith Geiger, NEA President
(quoted in USEPA, Radon in Schools, updated April 24, 2007)

Part III

What Can We Do As Parents for the Short Term and for the Long Term Improvement?

Chapter 10

System Overhaul: Developing Healthy Schools

Now that we have a better understanding of the hidden dangers within our schools, it's time to look at the other side of the coin, to identify what makes a school a safe place for our children; a place where learning is deep, where our children thrive, and where our children want to be. One might ask, "Are safe, vigorous, dynamic schools even a possibility in this day and age?" Such schools are not only possible, but many of our schools only need a bit of fine-tuning to correct the hidden dangers. I believe healthy school climates can occur in all schools, public or private, large or small, wealthy or those on limited budgets.

Indeed some successful schools already exist! Well then, does this mean there is already a perfect school which can be held up as a model for others to strive to achieve? The answer to this question is a definite yes and no! Yes, there are some dynamic healthy schools from which we can learn the necessary elements that make up such a climate, but since each school is unique the model must be tailored to "fit" each school community.

We know the changes must be based upon solid research and will take time and effort. However, we must keep in mind that even small improvements can have a significant impact upon the school culture, which can lead to more substantial and permanent changes. Every thoughtful and well-planned change can move students and schools toward the realization of a vibrant school climate.

ESTABLISHING A FRAMEWORK

In chapter one I asked the question: "What possibly can be so unique and work so successfully at some schools that students cannot wait to get to school, experience a sense of community and shared responsibility, and where learning is both broad and deep in scope?" It's time to answer this question with the development of an adaptable framework for schools to use to identify hidden dangers and to make the necessary changes.

Let's begin by restating our working definition of school climate. School climate refers to the unique combination of intellectual, behavioral, social, political, ethical and physical characteristics of the setting. In a healthy school climate these six elements are in balance. Since all schools are dynamic places it should be understood that in reality these elements are in constant flux, but we strive to reach the optimal school climate where these characteristics are in harmony. In order for these elements to be balanced we need a solid foundation upon which we build our school climate.

This foundation establishes that the basic needs of children will be the guiding principles upon which all policies and practices are built. These essential needs include:

1. The need for ongoing, nurturing relationships.
2. The need for physical protection, safety, and regulation.
3. The need for experiences tailored to individual differences.
4. The need for developmentally appropriate experiences.
5. The need for boundaries, structure, and expectations.
6. The need for stable, supportive communities and cultural continuity.
7. The need for protecting the future . . . maintaining and supporting growth.
(Brazelton & Greenspan, 2000)

We have seen that many schools only give lip service to addressing these needs. While some schools meet them better than others do, there is room for improvement in all schools. So, the next building block in our foundation for a healthy school climate is to address the basic needs of children through an open-minded, non-defensive reflection of each school. The need for transparency in our educational systems is vital to overcoming these hidden dangers.

Transparency involves a process of reflection and flexibility that is free of intimidation; this allows for identification of problems. Hidden dangers can be straightforwardly identified, analyzed and corrected in such a system. School personnel must be willing and able to look at established practices and beliefs from a multitude of perspectives.

When some students are not being served well, the policies and practices of the system should readily be questioned and changed without all the red tape and excessive time, energy and money it currently takes to make an appropriate educational intervention. Most importantly, change needs to occur without harm to the students and without the additional stress and time when lawyers are involved in the schools. The political and ethical elements need to be rebalanced when policies and practices are in need of adjustments which will impact all other elements within the school climate.

The third layer to our foundation is to create an atmosphere of optimism. To do this we need to turn our negative, pessimistic school environments into optimistic, flourishing places. The learning we desire for our children cannot take place in such pessimistic atmospheres. For example, schools must begin to look more for students' strengths, and to believe and trust that most students want to learn and succeed. When schools teach optimism to their students, teachers, and staff, the climate will then be one of hopefulness, allowing for the self-reinforcing sense of optimism to become well-established.

What was most striking about my research findings was the negative outlook perceived by parents and students in many of the schools. It was not until Scott, and a few of the other students, actually changed schools that they and their parents realized the differences between pessimistic and optimistic school climates. Most of the issues mentioned by parents involved negative comments made by teachers, administrators, coaches, and even lunchroom staff. These negative comments, attitudes and beliefs embody a disrespectful tone that no one should expect, even when visiting the IRS! Also, implied blame regarding learning and behavioral problems was placed on the student or on the family, and on the media. Certainly these factors can contribute; but school professionals too must acknowledge, or at least ask, what might be problematic within the schools which could be contributing to these issues. Parents must ask: "What can this school do differently to help my child learn?" Also, we must believe that there are ways to help and not give into the passivity of the times!

It also was quite remarkable to listen to and observe a total change in the tone of the students and parents when they spoke of the alternative school. Comments changed to a positive tone and included hopeful, controllable, workable solutions/situations. In the optimal schools children were not being diagnosed, parents were not being blamed, parents and children were listened to and helped to see that their input was valued. Children believed they could have an impact, and some control and influence over their learning. They felt unique and valued because the school's perspective appreciated their specific intelligences. Parents and children felt reassured that they were emotionally safe and understood. They had found a sense of community within a school with a balanced climate.

The good news is that optimism can be learned! Parents need to learn and model optimism for their children and we need to teach our administrators, teachers, and students to become honestly optimistic. This involves a way of thinking that flavors the environment in a positive manner ... not a

Pollyannaish manner. We can be both realistic and optimistic! In optimistic climates teachers and students have choices and control of their teaching and learning within an approved healthy curriculum. Change is seen as a welcomed opportunity, and "red tape" procedures and codes are not necessary.

In an optimistic, positive climate individuals will be viewed from the perspective of their strengths, not seen predominantly in terms of their weaknesses. Individual differences are valued, respected, indeed even celebrated, in such climates. We become one as a community respecting our uniqueness as human beings, all here for a very unique purpose, while clearly understanding that we are all more alike than we are different. Yet it is our very uniqueness that we must value fully, if we are to deeply learn and understand one another. With such a climate we are truly safer in our schools, in our communities, and such climates become self-fulfilling and sustainable!

This optimistic foundation leads us directly into the next essential foundation block: that of a strong, concerned, supportive administration with an open-door policy. It seems that all parents, educators, administrators, and even many of the children valued schools with open doors. School administrators must have the knowledge and skills to foster an open climate. Additionally, administrators and educators must be available and effective listeners. Students' and parents' concerns must be heard and addressed. So often it appears concerns are just dismissed, which tends to build anger.

Along these same lines, the mission of the school clearly reflects the practices in the school—and the practices and policies are based upon solid research. Mission statements need to be regularly reviewed, and updated right along with the continual process of reviewing, analyzing, and updating policies and practices . . . all based upon solid research.

The final building block of our optimal school climate involves the teachers. Teachers are the most essential factor in our schools (right next to the students)! Their importance cannot be overstated. We need teachers who are well educated and receive regular, ongoing, meaningful training. Teachers should not be asked to handle more than they are credentialed for and capable of managing, yet this is exactly what is happening in our schools. On any given day teachers may need to manage a vast array of problems. They need to be aware of and respect their own limitations and call, when needed, for professional assistance outside of the school without fear of reprimands. Specialized schools, educational consultants and pediatricians can and should be utilized more fully. These professionals and alternative schooling options can help resolve many problems for the school officials and most importantly for the children experiencing distress.

Teachers also must have high expectations for their students and we must have high expectations for our teachers. We cannot expect teachers to teach at a level of excellence if they are being asked to babysit a variety of serious problems. There are situations that call for different interventions to help out children in need. Such interventions must be readily flexible, readily available and agreeable to all involved.

Given a healthy, balanced school climate, I believe most teachers are capable of doing outstanding work with our children. When teachers know and believe they are truly doing good work with their students, then we will have teachers with high self-efficacy . . . an essential ingredient to a thriving school!

Right along these same lines we must understand that to get great teachers and keep them teaching our children, we are going to have to pay them adequately. Teachers contribute more to our world than most other professions combined.

"Teaching is the profession that teaches all other professions." (Unknown Author)

While we're on this issue of money I should explain that research findings concur that it does seem that smaller classes do matter. (Achilles, 1997; Blatchford, 2005) Also, for a more in-depth review of the federal class size policy, see the U.S. Government's policy on class size reduction which can be accessed through http://www.ed.gov/rschstat/eval/other/class-size/index.html However, this does not need to be a stumbling block for large urban schools. Many schools have successfully developed smaller communities within larger schools, each with its own unique identity. We must, however, work toward lowering the class size whenever possible, realizing that teachers can do a better job with more individualized attention with smaller groups.

CONFRONTING THE ISSUES

In chapter four we addressed the concealed damaging attitudes and assumptions. Our prime hidden danger is that we live in a nation of fear. This fear gets passed down to our children through many of our attitudes, assumptions, and procedures in the schools. We live in fear that our children will not get into the best preschools, that they will not get into Harvard, that they will not be able to keep up academically. We all want our children to be the best. This is only natural, but we have become so fearful for their well-being that many of the current practices are actually prohibiting successful academic progress.

As we could clearly see from case examples often times the attitudes, beliefs, and procedures which have become so ingrained in the schools just do not "fit," explain, or help all children. Indeed, some of the practices actually cause problems for many children, interfering with learning. For example, the movement toward measuring, assessing, and accountability has both its positive sides and negative consequences. It impacts teachers' ability to focus on essential curriculum and causes significant problems for many children.

Additionally, we saw that some curriculum choices can be harmful. We also can see that we need to make additional curriculum changes for constructive change. For example, certainly in the United States we should foresee the need for education to focus on foreign language acquisition. In a world as complex as ours surely we can see that the need for Americans to be able to understand and communicate with others from around the world is essential, yet this is not a serious focus in our schools! Clearly there are political, social, intellectual, behavioral and even ethical implications here which cause the school climate to be out of balance.

Also, there is such a misguided academic push toward getting more and more time for learning that such necessities like recess are being cut from the school day. This is not going to be helpful or healthy for children. It will negatively contribute to the obesity problem with children, and will not help them gain skills. Doing more of what already is not working is not helpful. Kids need to get out, run around, clear their heads so that academic time is used well.

Sports are also a vital part of healthy growing. Sports should be accessible to all children. It is essential to keep sports in balance too. The focus on competition, on winning at all costs is dangerous. Pushing kids to win at the expense of learning to know their limits is harmful. Pushing kids to the point of injury is wrong and unethical. Pushing kids to run faster to the point that they vomit is wrong; pushing kids to lose weight to wrestle, or cheer, or look better as a gymnast or skater is dangerous, unethical, even at times criminal. The violence we see in sports such as hockey and at times football and even soccer is alarming. Such practices reinforce violent behavior; indeed even condone it! This is a very dangerous practice! Finding a healthy balance with sports is essential.

Children also need to learn to eat healthy foods, in healthy amounts, and to pay attention to their own individual nutritional needs. Each child is different; some children need to eat much more than others and eat more often. This should not be a problem when individual needs are respected. Children also need to learn to pay attention to their own bodily signals, to understand their requirements for nourishment and other bodily functions. They need to learn about themselves just as much as they need to learn about math! This should be a natural process. By setting up hall passes and schedules for lunch where children only have 15–20 minutes to eat whatever they can does not set up a climate conducive to learning these necessary life skills. These hidden dangers set our kids up for eating disorders, including the serious crisis of childhood obesity. It's easy to see the imbalance with the physical, emotional, and basic needs not being met with these practices.

SYNTHESIS OF FOCUSED ISSUES

In chapter five we looked at toxic testing practices that unfairly discriminate against numerous children including those who may have learning differences, many boys due to gender differences in the classroom, students who may be "out of sorts" for a variety of reasons, students from various ethnic and cultural backgrounds, students from lower SES families and children who do poorly on traditional measures. We are discriminating against some of the most talented and creative students (our truly inductive deep learners) with harmful testing approaches. We know that testing in and of itself is a neutral process. However, when testing is misused it can become quite a dangerous process.

Instead, testing needs to be used to demonstrate areas in which students need more practice. Possibly teaching approaches need to be modified curriculum changed, or time given for more depth to learning through experiential learning. Ultimately testing should be composed of both authentic assessment (including portfolio assessment which can clearly demonstrate the learning and abilities of each student) along with more traditional forms of classroom testing and standardized testing USED FOR THE RIGHT REASONS! Testing should never be used as a threat to students or teachers; to do so is counterproductive. Misuse of testing puts the school climate out of balance intellectually, and most definitely ethically. We must always keep in mind that testing should not be a harmful process. It should be a helpful and ultimately an affirming process for the students and potentially for teachers as well!

So, let's put together our new understanding of what is needed for testing to be helpful and non-dangerous. First of all, additional research must be conducted on authentic assessment techniques. Although alternative approaches have been used to assess students for many years, there is little well-done research, including longitudinal studies, to demonstrate the effectiveness of such approaches. But this is true with conventional tests as well; studies done on more traditional testing approaches have not shown the damage done to many students because of the type of research conducted.

Each student becomes just a statistic and we cannot see the damaging effects . . . only that some students perform poorly, but not the reasons for these results. Computers allow us to crunch large numbers of statistics and come up with estimates (scores). However, it is imperative that those interpreting these numbers know the limitations of these scores and, most importantly, know how to help each student demonstrate his/her unique gifts, as well as addressing those areas that need more intensive instruction.

In chapter 6 we saw the damaging effects of labeling. Diagnosis does not belong in the schools; it needs to stay in the hands of our medical and psychological professionals. Teachers do not need a diagnosis in order to teach a child appropriately. They do need to know how to assess children for their strengths as well as their weaknesses and to appropriately interpret assessment measures in order to individualize an appropriate teaching strategy. Believe it or not, teachers receive very little training in the art and skills of assessment and testing! Undergraduate educational curriculums are so often tied up with meeting the often non-essential goals established by the State and Federal guidelines that essential knowledge and skills are not well addressed as part of their training!

Children also should be asked what might help them! So often input from the child is seen as pointless; yet they are the true experts on themselves. Furthermore, to consult with the child gives them a sense of control and responsibility for their learning. We must listen to our children. Here again we can see the negative impact of political policies that throw off the balance in our schools.

The increase in labeling and the diagnosis of specific disorders also was addressed in chapter 6. It appears that this increase involves the need to label somewhat quirky, bright kids who are poorly served within the traditional educational system. By labeling these children schools get more money for funding which so very often gets handed right over to the lawyers who should not be in the schools . . . at least not as often as they are currently! Lawyers may argue that it is because of lawsuits that change occurs, but in very few cases is this accurate. Certainly such cases as Brown vs. the Board of Education have been life changing for many students. However, the day-to-day cases do nothing but take time and money away from needed programs and make the lawyers richer! We can, and need to, use this educational money more effectively.

It seems obvious that children's individual needs are not being met in many instances (individual differences are not being respected) and the balance within the school climate is disrupted in several areas including ethics. Labels can also interfere with children socially, behaviorally, intellectually, and psychologically.

In chapter 7 we addressed the hidden dangers of unintentional gender inequity in our schools. Again here we have seen problems with meeting the individual needs of children (male or female), and not addressing their unique differences in terms of development as well. Boys and girls develop differently; not just in the obvious physical ways, but in their cognitive abilities as well. Boys and girls may well need to learn different curriculum, delivered in a different manner, at different times. We saw the gender divide in our schools from research and in case studies. Clearly, we can see that there are gender issues that need to be addressed! The causes of these gender discrepancies are multi-faceted and involve society's perceptions of boys, educational expectations, new state and federal testing policies, school climate, psychological/ emotional differences, and brain-based and biological differences (Connell & Gunzelmann, 2004; Gunzelmann & Connell, 2006).

Let's take a closer look at what can be done to help establish a healthier school climate for the gender issues. First of all, we need to confront our own understanding of both boys and girls and their unique strengths and needs. Second, we need to become much more accepting of individual differences; it may be accurate to say that more boys than girls have difficulty sitting still and coloring within the lines than girls, but it can be damaging to see only the typical scenarios or to stereotype. We must fully understand the uniqueness of each child. Both boys and girls should be assisted in understanding that we all learn differently and our learning should be based upon all of our unique contributions to the learning environment . . . not upon competition and who can color the neatest or do their math facts the fastest!

We also need to help all children, regardless of gender, to develop real friendships and to transcend the cliques which are based upon popularity, not a true sense of companionship and caring. Along these same lines, students need to be taught problem-solving approaches to acquiring social skills and to understanding one another. Boys should not be pushed to grow up too fast. They should be understood as having similar needs as girls for nurturing and close caring relationships, particularly at times when they most need it—into their teen years and older. All issues of diversity must be handled in a manner that provides an optimal learning environment for all students apart from gender, race, socio-economic level, or any other factor that may impact the learning of the child.

The issues discussed in chapter 7 can put the school climate out of balance by not addressing children's basic needs for individualized instruction which is appropriately based upon developmental levels, along with setting an atmosphere that is not at all helpful for boys who may experience difficulties socially, behaviorally, and intellectually. Clearly, there are ethical issues when a school does not address the gender discrepancies seen in the schools.

In chapter 8 we addressed issues of safety policies, including zero tolerance and lockdowns, and issues of school-related violence, including bullying and cliques. It seems apparent that the atmosphere in the schools is one of anxiety and heightened vigilance related to the fear that has taken over our nation. The schools too have played right into this hysteria. It will not be until we look at schools as places that are to be child-focused—not "Big Brother" focused—places where children can be playful, be inquisitive, truly be children again that we will see many forms of school violence subside.

It seems that school policies reflect an attitude of distrust toward our children; not expecting them to behave appropriately. These policies appear to expect kids to act out, to bully others and to be violent. This expectation can become the norm if we are not careful. If children begin to believe that violence is anticipated, then such behavior may become more typical, more normal in the eyes of our children. They will become even more desensitized to the cruelty in our society.

The media already does much too much desensitizing of our children regarding violent behavior. Certainly we do not want our schools unintentionally playing into this process! The money, time and effort spent on preparing for catastrophes is a real danger that focuses our children into believing that they truly are not safe! These issues can put our child's basic needs at risk, along with social ethical, intellectual, political, and behavioral areas out of balance on our school climate chart.

In chapter 9 we took a closer look at problems within the actual physical school buildings which can be quite unsafe and disruptive to the well being and education of our children and to school personnel as well. Obviously our older school buildings should meet basic safety guidelines for air quality, water quality, and building codes. Additionally, the land and materials used for building, remodeling and renovations need to be chosen with the long-term well-being of our children and all school personnel in mind.

Green building practices should be utilized whenever possible. Green schools are often called high performance school because they use safe, natural materials and operate in an efficient and ecological manner. Furthermore, green schools "protect occupant health, provide a productive learning environment, connect students to the natural world, increase average daily attendance, reduce operating costs, improve teacher satisfaction and retention, and reduce overall impact to the environment" (Global Green USA, 2006).

Classroom design and organization must also be considered. Why not have a classroom without desks or at the very least where children are not so restricted by rules about staying in their seats? Children need to get up and move around. Students in such settings are happier and healthier. Researchers at the Mayo Clinic believe that such classrooms will engage our future schools (Mayo Clinic, 2006). Furthermore, furniture should be comfortable and moveable to accommodate changing needs.

Even with routine maintenance of our schools we must monitor and adopt the least toxic approach. Hazardous chemicals, including those used for cleaning and pest management, should be eliminated. Parents and school personnel should be informed of any chemicals being used, and where and when applications are taking place. Unnecessary use of harmful chemicals should not be used merely for aesthetic reasons such as lawn care or for any other unnecessary usage.

All schools, whether old or new, should undergo regular, professional monitoring for all potentially harmful issues. The results should be researched and analyzed, and changes made as should be done with all dangers in the schools. Any necessary changes should be made by professionals trained to handle such problems. This area fits under basic needs, but also impacts the physical and ethical areas unbalancing the entire climate for all students and school personnel.

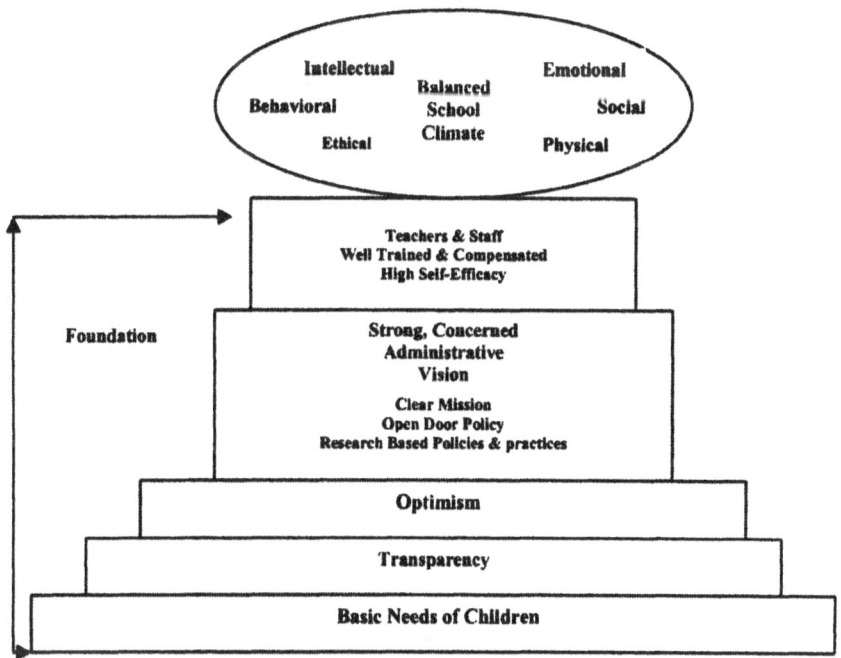

Figure 10.1. A School Free of Hidden Dangers: A Balanced School Climate

Chapter 10

SUMMARY IN A NUT SHELL

So, in a nut shell, parents should look for an optimal, healthy and safe school climate, free from hidden dangers with the following balanced elements illustrated in figure 10.1:

In a safe and healthy school climate we see choices, balance, alternatives, and a belief in the inherent goodness of people to want to do their best work when the circumstances support self-actualizing behavior. Children want to go to school; they experience a sense of belonging and achievement. All aspects of the school climate seem to be in reasonable balance (intellectually, socially, emotionally, behaviorally politically and ethically.). Children's most basic needs are met in an optimistic atmosphere.

School is a large part of our lives and the lives of our children. It should be a place we all want to go and spend our time, where we feel valued and appreciated too. Then the school offers a very optimal learning climate, a climate and a sense of belonging that even the most difficult circumstances outside of the school cannot break down. The school free from hidden dangers offers a way to have a very real impact on our youth, despite the current problems we are seeing in our culture. Let's see how we can transcend these hidden dangers and keep our schools thriving, safe, self-reinforcing!

> The culture may advertise its famous melting pot slogan, but everyone knows the true melting pot is the classroom and playground, where every variety of integration of turf and difference, not to mention every dynamic of the lower brain stem and cerebral cortex, has to be worked out.
>
> —Tom Cottle, 2004

Chapter 11

Transcending Dangers: Improvements for All Children

It's time to transcend the Hidden Dangers in our schools. We know what we need for the climate of all schools to be free of hidden dangers, but how do we implement these identified necessities and how do we maintain an optimal school climate without falling back into the hidden dangers vicious cycle? To transcend the hidden dangers trap we need to break the negative vicious cycle and generate a positive, dynamic and self-sustaining cycle of reflection, research, analysis and change.

TRANSCENDING HIDDEN DANGERS

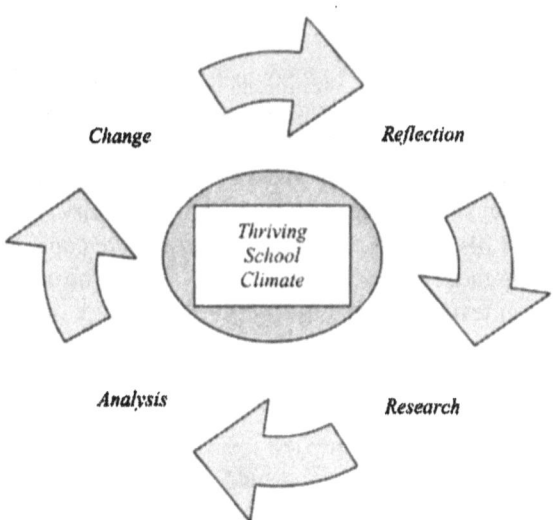

Figure 11.1. A Dynamic, Self-Sustaining Cycle for Thriving Schools for All Children

I do believe that at the very heart of most schools there are concerned administrators and teachers. Most of our school faculty and employees want to make a positive contribution to the lives of our children, but they get bogged down in red tape and long-established approaches. Administrators, teachers, parents, children and community must work together to reflect upon the hidden issues within *their* schools, carefully gathering and reviewing the related research, analyzing, then making needed changes, and regularly reflecting and revising when necessary . . . it truly will be a self-sustaining cycle.

Now we have a plan for a balanced, self-reinforcing, sustainable, optimal and safe school climate and we can make it a reality for all children! We can now make our schools places where children and teachers thrive from the excitement and challenge that true learning inspires.

IN THE INTERIM

Schools can and will change. We have many dedicated, hardworking, well-intentioned professional in our schools. But change takes time; sometimes it takes longer than we can wait, particularly if it is our child that is suffering. We need to support our educational institutions by awakening our educators to view problems within our schools from a different perspective; by redesigning our schools from the foundations of the buildings (in some cases) to the very core of the educational process in many of our schools.

It's going to take time, research, effort and courage to challenge current educational systems plagued by hidden dangers. We know from history that educational institutions are among the slowest to change. There is no doubt that we need to begin this process. However, in the meantime there are many children who are caught up in the fallout from hidden dangers and change may not come soon enough. Their futures are at risk. Many children will not attain the skills needed to become who they are capable of becoming if we do not help them immediately to obtain an education free of hidden dangers. So, in the meantime, while we begin the process of correcting the problems inherent in our schools, we also need to assist our children with transcending the immediate hidden dangers so no further harm is done to any child.

All children deserve a chance to revive their desire to learn and the opportunity to attend schools that are free from hidden, self-defeating problems. We all have encountered youth who do not care about their education, who have so many problems including poverty, homelessness, family and societal problems.

It's understandable that academic issues may not be first on the list of priorities for these children. Yet if we can make our schools safe, desirable places we can help these students as well, to transcend their most difficult life challenges.

We can and must make schools into places free from hidden dangers which impede the development of a vibrant school climate (which can immunize them from harmful outside influences). And so, we allow and encourage them to grow, learn and cope with difficulties in a manner that will enable them to successfully negotiate our complex society, and to contribute, when they are grown and ready, in a positive manner to the next generation. We cannot afford to lose a significant part of our younger generation to the apathy we are seeing in our schools, a reflection of the larger society.

We must help all students now to transcend these hidden dangers to reconnect with their interest in learning, their creativity, and with their belief in themselves to be able to do great things. We need to believe in our children, and to be strong enough not to let these hidden dangers overpower our children's desire to learn. We must realize that the cases presented in this book are of children who were seen as the problems. Yet most of these children had no diagnosis of learning disabilities, attention problems or primary psychological disorders. These were children who were poorly understood and most definitely underserved by their schools . . . children similar to your child. Yet, we can clearly see that the children were NOT the problem; however, certain school policies, practices and societal beliefs contribute to the educational crisis.

In turn parents and teachers were blaming their kids, compounding the children's difficulties. I do believe that these dangers are in part related to the increase in depression, anxiety, and other disorders that we are seeing with our youth! These kids cannot wait for our schools to improve their climates. They need change now!

In the meantime, while we await these constructive educational changes, we need options for our children. At these times it is important to know we have choices. We can turn to other resources including alternative education approaches such as charter schools, free schools, home schooling, e-schooling and a variety of hybrid educational approaches. Sometimes it takes an immediate change to save a child from a toxic school climate. In some cases all it takes is a change to a school that fits the child. Children such as Scott, Nicholas, Adam, Sally, Luke and all the cases we have seen deserve our help too. Oftentimes, all we need in the meantime to help these students transcend the hidden dangers is a change in approach or even a change in school. Choices and options are essential to transcending the hidden dangers in schools.

A variety of schools and approaches should be available to all children. A one-size-fits-all approach can no longer be tolerated by parents or teachers. There are too many children who are being compromised, being robbed of developing their potential to the fullest. They are being prevented from becoming who they were meant to be. Advances in technology afford us many unique opportunities to meet the needs of all students. For example, Scott in the case presented earlier discovered that he did much better when allowed to take computerized versions of traditional tests. Other technological advances have allowed us to work with E-portfolios with many added benefits. Storage of materials is much easier, many reviewers can assess students' material online for a more complete evaluation, and students can do the work of preparing and presenting their own portfolio, thus cutting the cost and time required to do other forms of assessment.

Alternative approaches to education are also becoming more available because of technological advances including: e-schooling and a variety of hybrid forms of distance learning. These are opening alternative educational possibilities to all children—children such as Sally and Carol, but also children in the most remote areas of the world where teachers and schools may not be available. Each child is unique and we must approach each child with respect, caring and awe. We have a lot to learn from each child. Let's help these kids become who they were meant to be by getting rid of these hidden dangers in our schools!

Teachers too must have options and choices in order to rise above the inherent problems in schools. There are too many teachers who lose their idealism after their first few years of teaching; they give up trying to make the impact they intended. Alternative education approaches empower our teachers, reawakening their desire, the passion that sent many of our best teachers into the field in the first place! We cannot sit idly by any longer waiting for this to occur. Teachers can make a difference starting today! Small changes within the classroom can make all the difference in the world to a child who is floundering. Teachers can begin by making little changes within their classroom while the administrators are attempting to make larger-scale changes within their schools.

In order to transcend these hidden dangers within our schools we need to continue to conduct well-planned research within our schools and to keep up with the cutting edge research on children from a multidisciplinary perspective. And most importantly we need to be outspoken when we see things in our schools that are troubling, even when that's how things have always been done, or when it goes against the grain of public policy. In order to do our best work, to help our children thrive, we must not tolerate mediocre education—we need choices for our children and teachers NOW! These choices must be made readily available for all students and free of stigma and labels. Such alternatives also must be fully supported by our school personnel and seen as respected options to meet the needs of all students. In Chapter 12 we will take a more in-depth look at your options for your academically struggling child.

Chapter 12

Options/Alternatives for Parents of Kids Struggling in Our Schools

So, now that you know the hidden dangers that can sabotage your child's learning, what are your options to help your academically struggling child? Navigating these hidden problems can be tricky, but there are ways to help your child.

As you are quite aware by now, a one-size-fits-all approach to education does not work for many children. When beginning to look for alternatives it is important to take into consideration your child's personality. Is he/she a child that can work well independently? Does she/he need structure? Are traditional schools a better choice or are schools that are more flexible in nature preferred? Are time limits important or do such limits interfere with your child's learning? Are small classes/schools better for your child? What about individual one-on-one attention? Does your child want an active social life including clubs and sports? What about food options . . . does the school provide healthy choices? Is the school building safe and free of toxins?

Clearly, there are many issues to consider . . . but you are an expert on your child! And do not hesitate to ask your child for input into the decision-making as well. After all it is he/she that has to deal with the day-to-day reality of the choice. First and foremost remember you are your child's best advocate and you are well on your way to getting the help he/she needs. You already have taken a huge step in learning about the subtle problems that exist in many schools and, as you know, some children are more adversely affected than others.

Initially you should set up an appointment with your child's teacher and let him/her know how you understand the conflicts that interfere with learning. The school psychologist or school counselor may be an excellent resource to help you as well. You will be able to ascertain from these meetings if the school personnel are willing to work seriously with you to make schooling successful for your child. For example, if your child has serious allergies and asthma from molds within the building and the school professionals are only suggesting they vacuum more often and change the sponges used for cleaning, I think you can safely say that these are not serious attempts to remedy the toxic mold situation in the school building. However, a good rule of thumb to remember is that it is the best route to work with the school personnel whenever possible. Most school administrators, psychologists, counselors and teachers do want to help if they can.

Yes, you could file a lawsuit against the school to make the necessary repairs, and probably you should. It will help all the children in the long run, but your child cannot wait! It may take extensive time for the town to put aside money from their budgets to make such repairs . . . and time is of the essence with your child's education. Possibly the school administration will be willing to make a change of schools to another healthy building within the district. And be careful not to let the administration blame the problem on your child. After all, it is the building that is sick . . . not your child!

Realize that you do not have to go it alone into such school meetings. Oftentimes parents feel as if they have become a child again in such meetings; they feel intimidated and powerless. There are *educational lawyers* to help, although they usually come with a high price tag. Another option involves an *advocate*. Many areas have advocacy groups where individuals experienced in negotiating for children's needs can assist you. One caution however, at times I have seen these individuals go in with a chip on their shoulders . . . using a demanding approach rather than one of negotiation with educators. This sets the stage for an adversarial process rather than an informative session and a shared desire to help the child learn. So, be aware of this inclination. With careful screening you can find an excellent advocate since many are quite experienced and skilled at getting the child's needs met!

Ideally it is usually best if the child can stay in his/her school and classroom. Children can learn a lot about negotiating and adapting in life's situations by staying in their classroom when possible. This way they do not have to be uprooted from their friends and adjust to a new setting. However, as we have seen from the many cases throughout this book there are times when it is best to change the child's teacher/classroom or even school setting. If the teacher is not willing to work with you and your child, you may have to make a change in classrooms or even schools. If the building does not meet specific health needs you may need to find a different school. Or there may even be times when your child has been bullied or ostracized to the point that a change in locations is warranted. The decision to make a change in schools should be taken seriously and used when other options are not feasible or readily available.

PHILOSOPHY OF EDUCATION

If you do choose to change your child's school, then what are some alternatives? First of all, you should always check on the genuineness of the school, its mission, and choice of curriculum. All teachers and professional educators should be fully certified and schools accredited. Also, it helps to know your own beliefs about education . . . your educational philosophy. I will explain my educational philosophy here so that you can get an idea of what is involved. My philosophy of education has developed over more than a quarter of a century. When I was an undergraduate student back in the mid-1970s I first began to think about my teaching philosophy. I had read many different philosophies and they all sounded reasonable on paper. However, it was not until I actually started teaching and working as a psychologist with children experiencing learning challenges that having a philosophy of teaching became very important to me.

I discovered early on that my beliefs about teaching had to fit both my teaching style and meet the needs of my students. So, to make a long story short, here is my philosophy of teaching: I believe that I follow a constructivist approach to teaching and learning. Constructivist viewpoints are firmly grounded in the research of Piaget, Vygotsky, and Gestalt psychologists, as well as educators including Bruner and Dewey. A constructivist approach involves the student taking an active role in building or constructing their understanding of the content, issues, and learning process.

Additionally I believe that behavioral, cognitive, and social cognitive perspectives on learning all add to our understanding of learning. They need to be well understood in order to be adapted and applied effectively with students. A student's perception of learning is crucial to successful outcomes as is the social learning environment. School climate can enhance or seriously impede learning. (My research and writing in this book illustrate my beliefs by example.)

Naturally, I present essential material, but I also require the students to be actively involved in their learning. Students must be engaged in thought, discussion, interaction, research and debate which allows for higher level mental processing and the consideration of multiple perspectives. I use an inquiry and problem-based learning approach where students are required to formulate hypotheses, collect data, draw conclusions, and then to reflect back upon the original questions and the process of problem solving and critical thinking skills. I also strongly believe in experiential learning environments where students go out into the field to test out their newly found theories and ideas.

Consideration of students' learning styles and utilizing a variety of assessment strategies is another part of my teaching beliefs. In addition to traditional assessment approaches I use alternative assessment strategies including portfolio assessment which affords a healthy balance to student evaluation. Test scores and grades can be a part of portfolio assessment and should be if they are used appropriately ... i.e. in order to determine which knowledge or skills are in need of further strengthening and what content has been mastered and can now be built upon to deepen learning. (For more information regarding these educational issues you may want to refer to Woolfolk, 2006.)

So now, what do you think is essential for learning? You know your child best and if one educational approach is not working well, it may be time to try another.

TYPES OF SCHOOL OPTIONS

So, now let us take a look at the different types of schools that are based upon varying theories, philosophies, and approaches designed to meet the needs of diverse children. Learn about the schools and their approaches, visit the schools and spend some time observing in the classrooms before making a decision to start your child in a new setting. Just reading about a school's mission is not enough, you must be able to ascertain if they actually put their mission statement into practice. Although this is not by any means an exhaustive list of different options in schooling, I want to present to you some of the more basic underlying concepts and configurations in schooling.

Let us take a look at the private school options. First there are a variety of private school choices. One such choice includes *independent schools* which are nonprofit schools. Each independent private school has its own unique educational mission. But they share the common commitment to provide a safe environment in which young people can learn academic skills **plus** the importance of hard work, leadership, personal responsibility, and good citizenship according to the National Association of Independent Schools. (There is a link included in the resource Appendix for the National Association of Independent schools which has a listing of all member schools.)

Parochial and religious-based schools are private schools as well. These schools usually offer a more traditional, structured education along with the teaching of a specific religious doctrine. Tuition is charged, although sometimes the tuition is less than many other private schools. Teachers can be lay persons or clergy who may not be trained educators. (The Council for American Private Education has a large list of such schools.)

There also are numerous special education private schools as well, but these are for students that have a documented disability. (Possibly some of the alternative approaches and school discussed in this book may work well for some of these students too.) These private specialized schools can be accessed from a link in the resource appendix for those parents interested in these schools.

Then there are the college preparatory day and boarding schools offering another possible private school option for some children. These are numerous in number; some quite prestigious and expensive, others less exclusive, but highly academically oriented. Theses schools may have a more traditional focus on academics for academics sake . . . and for the distinct purpose of scoring well on tests and gaining admission to more prestigious higher-level institutions. (These can be pressure-cooker environments for some students, while others may thrive in this atmosphere.)

Then there are the proprietary schools. These are private schools that operate for a profit. Currently there are schools from only seventeen states that are members of NIPSA National Independent Private School Association. These schools are run by educators first and reportedly many of the goals and objectives are the same as many private and public schools.

One of the problems with private school education is that it is out of reach for many children because of the cost. Some well-endowed private schools are able to give "worthy students" financial assistance. (What student is not worthy?) At any rate private school is not always an option. So, what are the other choices for parents who can not afford a private school education? Well, there are still many.

Charter schools are one possibility. By definition charter schools are *nonsectarian public schools* offering options to children. Oftentimes such charter schools operate with less restrictions that pertain to more conventional public schools (uscharterschools.org). As such charter schools are frequently started by parents, teachers, administrators, community leaders or local organizations that are dissatisfied with the more traditional public school.

Such schools can provide education from kindergarten right on up through grade twelve. In turn charter schools are accountable to their sponsors, to the parents and to the funding source (USDOE). Charter schools can have more freedom from rules that can impede learning as we have seen in this book. But parents still must be careful in choosing a charter school that fits their child. All charter schools still must demonstrate adequate learning or risk losing their charter to operate. A list of your state's charter schools can be found by accessing your state's Department of Education. A link to all states' DOE is included in the Resources Appendix for your convenience.

A *magnet school* has some differences from a charter school. Magnet schools are bureaucratically a part of the public school system (they share the same administration). In these schools students are usually zoned or placed based upon the location of the school they reside most closely to, but the magnet school usually offers some special mode of instruction such as a Montessori magnet or a magnet that specializes in the arts to name just a few. Magnet schools may receive additional funding to enable them to spend more money on their students, supplies, teachers, and programs.

Virtual Learning Academies are another newer alternative. These schools offer a structure of distance learning where part or all of the instruction is provided using technology and the student is not at the same location as the instructor according to NCES. I have found these newer alternatives to be quite an exciting option for a full time program or for students to just pick up a course or two. Many states now have *free tuition to public virtual learning academies*. Additionally, the teachers may be both content and teaching experts.

My brief experience with this approach to date has been quite positive. Since children grow up with computers today this format can be a natural fit for so many. It also offers unique assessment approaches which can help students learn to see testing as an important part of learning. Pretests show what they do not yet know . . . post test can show what they still may need to focus more upon, and if there are any particular areas that still need further work. This allows the student to go at his own pace and rework areas that may have been problematic before moving on. Gaps in learning will be far less of a problem and students can learn to use testing in a positive way . . . and this approach can help to reduce test anxiety since children have more control over the process and their learning. Testing becomes a helpful tool used in this manner.

Homeschooling has become a very practical alternative for many families. Originally it was seen as religious-based, and there were biases that homeschooled children were socially less capable. Interestingly enough, current research on homeschooled children indicates that these children can receive a superior education, are very well adjusted, and are being accepted into the most prestigious colleges and universities. Many of these children have learned how to learn; they enjoy learning, think more deeply, and overall are less stressed than the regular school counterparts. For a more detailed account of home schooling please see Bielick, Chandler, and Broughman (2001).

According to the U.S. Department of Education, a child is considered to be a homeschooled student when parents report their child as being educated at home rather than a public or private school and as long as their involvement in school did not exceed twenty-five hours per week, and if they were not at home due to a temporary illness. Homeschooling is a legal option to attendance in public or private school and is in accordance with Chapter 279:2, laws of 1990. It used to be the choice of parents from specific religious preferences. Christian homeschooling programs are plentiful and offer unique, individual education for families. Yet homeschooling today is no longer reserved for students with specific beliefs . . . it is a valuable resource for many children and for a variety of reasons.

Since 1999 homeschooling has increased dramatically. As of 2003 the number of homeschooled children in the U.S. was estimated to be 1,096,000. This is a 29 percent increase from the estimated 850,000 home schooled students in 1999 according to. (Bielick, S., Chandler, K., & Broughman, S.P. (2001); *Homeschooling in the United States: 1999* (NCES 2001–033); Washington, DC: National Center for Education Statistics.) This figure has only grown since 2003 as more and more parents realize that their children are being underserved and in some cases even failed by our schools.

Homeschooled children can also be part homeschooled and still attend the local public school for a part of the day, as well and take extra curricular activities and team sports. I also believe it is important to have your homeschooled child involved in community service work. It's important to feel a sense of connection to one's community and neighbors. There are often programs available for homeschooled children at the YMCA and at local bookstores and libraries too.

Assessment with homeschooled children can offer many options as well. Portfolio assessment can help children learn to take responsibility for their learning while reducing anxiety levels. Such alternative assessment approaches allow the child to feel a sense of ownership and control over their learning and can incorporate both standardized assessment and demonstrations of actual work. Testing can be used in more beneficial ways. It can be used as a study tool, a way to allow students to see how much they have learned, what needs to be reinforced and to correct their mistakes. Traditional tests never allow for the constructive use of well-designed tests ... the scores are entered in as a grade and the student does not learn what he/she has not yet mastered.

Homeschooling can have added benefits of helping children get the rest they need ... no longer do they need to get to the school bus by 6:30 AM and they can eat and exercise in a more balanced manner. Their time can be used more effectively, and the responsibility for learning is placed more squarely on the shoulders of the student. Maturity is developed along with a sense of mastery, responsibility, belief in one's abilities, and goals for the future.

A personal account of a hybrid home school approach used with an adolescent student is recounted in the following case of Tommy. As usual, names and identifying information have been changed.

> Tommy's was home schooled for his eighth and ninth grades of schooling. His parents made a complete change of view regarding this schooling option. They report that this approach fit Tommy's needs to a tee. Since beginning the home schooled program they observed the following positive changes in Tommy. He became motivated to read, write, and study again. In fact, there

were numerous times when they have had to tell him to stop reading, writing, or studying! He seemed happier, took part more readily in family conversations, and even expressed concern over community issues. This was a remarkable transformation considering he felt very discouraged before changing to this home schooled approach.

No doubt such changes may be due to several factors, but his parents believe the improvements were in large part the result of this hybrid learning program, encouraging student responsibility and allowing for schedule flexibility. Tommy was no longer disrupted in his learning by having to change classes every hour or so. Instead he was able to focus in-depth on each subject for as long as necessary to gain competence. His parents report that he had no trouble staying focused for extended periods of time when not disrupted by the regular daily school schedule. Tommy's learning was both broad and deep in scope and he was intrinsically motivated to keep researching each assignment and topic covered.

The use of technology was very helpful for Tommy as well. He was able to communicate with his teachers efficiently, receiving helpful and timely feedback when necessary. Tommy began saving his online conversations with his instructors for future reference. This can easily be done and became a valuable resource to him when he needed to refer back for instructional purposes and allowed parents to oversee the depth of his learning. He also was able to use the internet, and learned to use it well. The ability to ascertain solid research sources was mastered. (He even learned how to do genealogy research which he found fascinating.) Additionally, the computer was an ideal way for Tommy to keep his work organized. No longer did parents or teachers see the messy locker, but instead he had well organized computer files.

A hybrid approach to home schooling also allowed Tommy to do extra curricular activities for which he previously did not have time. For example, he became an active community volunteer and engaged in experiential learning. Community work became an integral part of his life, helping him to become a responsible community member. Even physical education improved too! His parents were concerned that Tommy was not getting enough exercise having PE only one quarter a year in his traditional school curriculum, .With the home school approach he became active with other home schooled children at the local YMCA, participated in a community golf camp, walks and rides his bike and also was involved with one of the junior varsity teams at the local high school.

There were other noticeable improvements as well. For example, even Tommy's nutrition improved! He ate healthy food at meal time and was able to get healthy snacks whenever he needed. Tommy reportedly needs more food than most kids. He is a thin young man and would lose his focus if hungry. (His pediatrician encouraged him to eat healthy food as much as he wanted.) Even the family had more time to enjoy a wider variety of activities, including attending local concerts. Tommy included a couple of the brochures in his portfolio since has gained an interest and appreciation of classical music.

Tommy's parents wanted to make sure that this approach was keeping pace with the more traditional school program. They wanted to make sure that he was learning the material necessary and thus decided to use both portfolio assessment and a standardized testing approach to ensure attainment of learning outcomes. They found that the home schooling was working well; Tommy was making academic gains that surpassed his peers.

Overall, Tommy's parents were quite impressed with this hybrid home schooling approach to learning. It was definitely right for their son. Tommy realized he had to take responsibility for his learning and whether or not he succeeded was up to him. He became a self-motivated, reliable and confident learner. In fact, he expressed concern about the summer months and does not want to stop! What a change had occurred in this young man.

Additionally, there are even more options possible available to your child. For advanced students, community colleges or local colleges may allow your child to audit or even take a course for credit. Of course this can cost money, but can be an added boost to your child's confidence if college professors, teachers, and tutors may be available to work one on one as a tutor for your homeschooled child as well. Since technology is improving, and resources are becoming more readily and financially available, there are many more alternatives out there just waiting to be discovered.

SO IN A NUTSHELL

1. *Try your best to work with your child's school.* Make an appointment and go in with a supportive, but well-researched attitude.
2. Go to your *state's Department of Education.* (You can visit in person by appointment or go to the website and discover many helpful resources and contact information.) See appendix re: resources.
3. If necessary, find out what *schooling options* are within your area as possibilities for your child. (Do not forget to check on their credentialing.)
4. Do you want to try *homeschooling* or a *hybrid* approach to educating your child? It is important to make sure your child's homeschooling program helps your child to master the basics, as well as deepens learning and enriches the options of content in more ways than can be offered within the child's current school.
5. Now you are ready to make an informed decision about your child's schooling. (Remember there are professionals available to help you if necessary.)
6. Monitor your child's progress. Your monitoring or assessment of progress should involve much more than grades and test scores. Is your child

interested in learning again? Is he/she more confident? Less anxious? Is there time and opportunity for interaction with other children? Is your child healthier? Is he/she getting enough exercise? Sleep? In other words, are your child's needs being met for optimal development better now than they were before? If so, how so? Be specific. Portfolio assessment can and should be used for all children to document progress in all areas that impact learning. These areas need to be met in order for your child to learning optimally.
7. Make adjustments/changes to your child's school program as needed based upon feedback from assessment and input from those professionals working with your child.
8. Enjoy, relax a bit and allow your child's love of learning to be reignited!

WHERE DO WE GO FROM HERE?

There is still more work to do, more research, more analysis, more useful assessment, more revisions of programs. This of course is an ongoing cycle to ensure a healthy learning environment for your child. We are making progress: progress toward educational excellence for all children, education free from hidden dangers, education where all children can have access to an education that "fits" their needs.

Parents, please remember the *ABC'S of getting your child's educational needs met:*

A = Advocate for your child
B = Believe in your child
C = Change what is necessary to change to get your child thriving in school and the **S** = support for your child
D = Don't give up on your child.

These are the ABC'S that can bring your child success in school.

Kids, you too need to believe in yourselves. Understand that you can learn given the right approaches, the right environment and the right attitude. Yes, your parents, teachers and schools are only a part of the answer. The most important part is you! Take control of your education and your future. You can do it! For where we go from here depends upon you!

Appendix

Annotated Resources

Parents may find the following annotated list of resources helpful when determining the appropriate approaches for their child. Please keep in mind that this is not an exhaustive list of resources, but it is a way to steer you in the direction of some of the more helpful professional resources. The internet is full of sites, some of which are not helpful and could actually be costly and detrimental. You may want to search some or all of the following:

Alternative Education Resource Organization: AERO is an outstanding resource for parents and educators. You can access the site by going to: http://www.educationrevolution.org or by the following contact methods.
Contact Information:
Address: 417 Roslyn Rd., Roslyn Heights, NY, 11577
E-mail: info@educationrevolution.org
Phone: (516) 621-2195
Fax: (516) 625-3257

CAPE Council for American Private Education. This site has information on the differences among many types of private schools, particularly the religious based schools. You can access this information by going to: http://www.capenet.org/schools.html.

Family Unschoolers Network is a resource that supports unschooling, home schooling and encourages self-directed learning. There are numerous resources for parents and students including events, conferences and a way to communicate with other unschoolers and home schoolers. You can access this information by going to: www.unschooling.org

F2be the Freedom to Be Natural Learners is a valuable resource that attempts to bring together people from countries world wide who believe that educational reform is needed. The F2be site has many worldwide resources that you may find interesting, helpful and informative. You can access f2be be going to www.f2be.com

HomeSchool.com: Here you will find a Home Schooling Resource Guide along with much other helpful information including curriculum for the home schooled child. You can access this information by going to Home School.com at: http://www.homeschool.com/resources/ConnectionsAcademy/default.asp.

iEARN International Education and Resource Network: is a non-profit international education resource network comprised of more than 25,000 schools from more than 125 countries! It allows educators and students to work together online. More information can be obtained from www.ieran.org

IPL: The Internet Public Library can be accessed at www.ipl.org and has numerous resources to assist parents with finding appropriate literature on alternative educational choices. IPL is a public library for the world wide web.

LDOnline is a website with outstanding resources for parents and educators involved with children with learning differences as well as learning disorders. You can access this information by going to: http://www.ldonline.org/

Magnet Schools of America offers support and leadership for public school choice programs. There is information about the magnet schools and conference information, but basically magnet schools offer choice for innovative education programs that are geared to increase educational equity, diversity, and academic excellence. Information can be accessed by going to: http://www.magnet.edu/index.php

National Association of Independent Schools. NAIS is the national voice for independent schools. Standards, resources and networking possibilities are available at: http://www.nais.org/ or Email: info@nais.org
Address: National Association of Independent Schools
1620 L Street NW, Suite 1100
Washington, DC 20036-5695
Telephone: (202) 973-9700
Fax: (202) 973-9790

NCACS: The National Coalition of Alternative Community Schools is a not for profit educational organization designed to assist parents, students and educators with alternative education. Information on home schooling, independent (private) alternative schools & programs, public alternative schools & programs, alternative colleges and a variety of alternative resources are available. You can access this information by going to: http://www.ncacs.org/ncacs.htm

NCES: National Center for Education Statistics is a government center with documentation of well conducted research available for your review. You can access this information by going to: http://nces.ed.gov/

NIPSA: National Independent Private School Association provides information on proprietary schools. These are schools run for profit that do not answer to a board of trustees. However, these schools employ professional educators and have similar missions statements and goals to many other schools. You can find out more about these proprietary schools by going to the following link. One may be right for your child! http://www.nipsa.org

Peterson's Private Schools and Boarding School Search can help you locate schools within your area. Go to: http://www.petersons.com/pschools/code/psector.asp Private School Finder can help you locate a variety of different types of private schools. This resource can be found by going to http://privateschool.about.com and searching within a particular state.

Private School Review also can assist you with your search for the right private school for your child. It can be accessed at: http://www.private-schoolreview.com/

The Child Advocate: National and State Child Advocacy Resources is an outstanding resource and can be accessed by going to: http://www.childadvocate.net/stateresources.htm Accessed 3/22/09.

The Independent School Directory is a valuable resource on information about independent schools This can be accessed at: http://www.independentschools.com/.

The Parent Advocacy Group for Educational Rights is a nonprofit organization created in response to the conditions in public schools. This group is located in Maryland and can be reached at: http://www.pagergroup.org/.

Unschooling.org. See Family Unschoolers Network in the above list.

US Charter Schools is another helpful site with numerous resources available. Go to: http://www.uscharterschools.org/pub/uscs_docs/o/definitions.htm. Also, President Obama has renewed his campaign pledge to support charter schools. He has called on states to lift the caps on the number of allowable chart schools. (CNN Politics, 2009).

U.S. Department of Education offers outstanding information and resources for parents of academically struggling children. You can contact the US Dept. of Education by going to: http://www.ed.gov/index.jhtml or by calling: 1-800-USA-LEARN (1-800-872-5327)

State Information: You can also find out specific information within your state by going to: http://www.ed.gov/about/contacts/state/index.html?src=gu

US Department of Education Institute for Education Sciences Search for Private schools Can be accessed at: http://nces.ed.gov/surveys/pss/privateschoolsearch/
This can offer valuable information to assist you with your private school search. See NCES above.

U.S. Dept. of Education: website is a valuable resource and a good starting place for parents to find out more about a variety of *education alternatives.* You can access this site by searching: http://nces.ed.gov/pubs2006/homeschool/. Spend time navigating this site. You can also link to your local state's Department of Education form this location.

You can also search on the web for Home School + your state. You will then have access to a number of resources including:

- Home schooling support groups
- Home schooling resources
- Home schooling laws

Make sure you contact your states Department of Education as well. Most states have home schooling pages within their website with resources including contact names and numbers, laws and administrative rules, policy & procedures, technical advisories, Home education Advisory Council, State Home Educators Associations, Grade Level Expectations, particular sites of interest and other resources available for parents of home schooled children. Example of NH State DOE Home Education Page go to: http://www.ed.state.nh.us/EDUCATION/doe/organization/curriculum/HomeEducation.htm

Virtual Schooling and home schooling are excellent educational formats for many children You can find more information available at: http://nces.ed.gov/pubs2006/homeschool/distancelearning.asp

A FINAL NOTE

Please understand that this is not an exhaustive list of resources, but should be very helpful in finding an appropriate educational choice for your child. Best wishes on your search and please contact me directly if I can be of further assistance. I can be reached at: b.gunzelmann@snhu.edu or through my website.

References and Suggested Readings

The following are sources I have used when writing this book. Many are referenced in the text of Hidden Dangers. All are worth reading to fully understand the issues involved.

Achilles, C. M. 1997. Small classes, big possibilities. *School Administrator* 54 (9): 6–9, 12–13.
Aiken, L. R. 2000. *Psychological testing and assessment.* Boston: Allyn & Bacon.
Alternative Education Resource Organization: AERO http://www.educationrevolution.org/ (accessed May 12, 2009).
American Bar Association. 2000. *Juvenile Justice Policies: Zero tolerance policy report.* ABA:
American Bar Association. 2000. (Quoted in W. Ayers, B. Dohrn, and R. Ayers, eds., 2001.) *Zero tolerance: Resisting the drive for punishment in our schools.* New York: The New Press.
American Psychiatric Association. 2000. *Diagnostic and statistical manual of mental disorders: DSM-IV-TR* (4th ed.) Washington, DC.
Asperger's Resource. http://www.aspergerresources.com/famous_people_with_aspergers.html (accessed May 16, 2007).
Ayers, W., B. Dohrn and R. Ayers. 2001. *Zero tolerance: Resisting the drive for punishment in our schools.* New York: The New Press.
Bandura, A. 1965. Influence of models' reinforcement contingencies on the acquisition of imitative responses. *Journal of Personality and Social Psychology* 1: 589–595.
Bandura, A. 1977. *Social learning theory.* New York: General Learning Press.
Baron-Cohen, S. 2003. *The essential difference: The truth about the male and female brain.* New York: Basic Books.
Basham, P. 2001. *Homeschooling: From the extreme to the mainstream.* Vancouver, BC, Canada: Fraser Institute.

Balsham, P., J. Merrifield, and C. R. Hepburn. 2007. Homeschooling: From the extreme to the mainstream.

Biederman, J., E. Mick, S.V. Faraone, E. Braaten, A. Doyle, T. Spencer, T.E. Wilens, E. Frazier, and M.A. Johnson. 2002. Influence of gender on Attention Deficit/Hyperactivity Disorder in children referred to a psychiatric clinic. *American Journal of Psychiatry* 159: 36–42.

Biederman, J., J. Newcorn, and S. Sprich. 1991. Comorbidity of attention-deficit/hyperactivity disorder with conduct, depressive, anxiety, and other disorders. *American Journal of Psychiatry* 148: 564–577.

Bielick, S., K. Chandler, and S. P. Broughman. 2001. *Homeschooling in the United States: 1999.* NCES 2001–033. Washington, DC: National Center for Education Statistics.

Black, S. 2004. Safe schools don't need zero tolerance. *Education Digest* 70(2): 27–31.

Blatchford, P. 2005. A multi-method approach to the study of school class size differences. *International Journal of School Research Methodology* 8 (3): 195–205.

Brazelton, T.B. and S.I. Greenspan. 2000. *The irreducible needs of children: What every child must have to grow, learn, and flourish.* Cambridge, MA: Perseus Publishing.

Brown v. Board of Education 1952, 1953, 1954. The Supreme Court of the United States. http://www.nationalcenter.org/brown.html (accessed May 31, 2007).

Children's Environmental Health Network. Sept. 5, 2005. *A child-safe U.S. chemicals policy.* Washington, DC: CEHN http://www.cehn.org/Education.html.

Civil Rights Project Harvard University. 2000. *Opportunities suspended: The devastating consequences of zero tolerance and school discipline.* http://www.civilrightsproject.harvard.edu/convenings/zerotolerance/synopsis.php (accessed May 30, 2007).

Civil Rights Project Harvard University. 2003. *Minority children with disabilities will be harmed in disproportionate numbers if IDEA's discipline safeguards are reduced or eliminated.* http://www.civilrightsproject.harvard.edu/policy/alerts/idea.php (accessed May 30, 2007).

Clinton, H. 2000. *New York Times,* April 6, 25. (accessed August 22, 2007) www.ontheissue.org/2008/Hillary_Clinton_Education.htm

CNN Politics.com. March10, 2009. *The 44th president first 100 days. Obama wants to overhaul education from 'cradle to career.'* http://www.cnn.com/2009/POLITICS/03/10/obama.education/index.html?section=cnn_latest (accessed March 14, 2009).

Collins, M. 1996. Documented on CBS "60 Minutes." www.enthink.com/quotations/teachers_and_teaching/ (accessed January 10, 2007).

Conlin, M. May 26, 2003. The New Gender Gap. *Business Week* 74–82.

Connell, D. September, 2002. Left Brain/Right Brain. *Instructor* 28–32, 89.

Connell, D. and B. Gunzelmann. 2004. The new gender gap: Why are so many boys floundering while so many girls are soaring? *Instructor* 113(6): 14–17.

References

Consumer Product Safety Commission CPSC. June 13, 2000. Release #00–123. *News from CPSC. cpsc releases test results on crayons: Industry to reformulate.* Washington, DC: Office of Information and Public Affairs. http://www.cpsc.gov/CPSCPUB/PREREL/prhtml00/00123.html (accessed May 29, 2007).

Coopersmith, S. 1967. *The antecedent of self-esteem.* San Franscico: Freeman.

Cottle, T. 2004. Feeling scared. *Educational Horizons* 83(1): 42–54.

Council for American Private Education CAPE. http://www.capenet.org/schools.html (accessed March 28, 2009).

Dalton, P. 1999. When Did We Lose Sight of Boys? *Washington Post*, May 9. http://www.illinoisloop.org/quotes.html#gender (accessed online January 10, 2007).

Darling-Hammond, L. 2008. Assessment for learning round the world: What would it mean to be internationally competitive? *Phi Delta Kappan* 90(4), 263–72D.

Einstein, A. www.enthink.com/quotations/teachers_and_teaching/ (accessed January 10, 2007).

Elkind, D. 1981, 1988, 2001. *The hurried child.* Cambridge, MA: DeCapo Press.

Estrada, I. (n.d.). www.enthink.com/quotations/techers and _teaching/ (accessed January 10, 2007).

Family Unschoolers Network. http://www.unschooling.org (accessed May 15, 2009).

Farberman, R. 2006. Zero tolerance policies can have unintended effects, APA report finds. *Monitor on Psychology* 37(9): 27.

F2be.com. *The freedom to be natural learners.* http://www.f2be.com/organisations.htm (accessed May 15, 2009).

Gardner, H. 1991. *The unschooled mind: How children think and how schools should teach.* New York: Basic Books

Gardner, H. 1999. *Intelligence reframed.: Multiple intelligences for the 21st century.* New York: Perseus.

Gardner, H., Csikszentmihalyi, M., and Damon, W. 2001. *Good work: When excellence and ethics meet.* New York: Basic Books.

Gates, B. 2005. Addressing the National Governors Association, February. http://www.nga.org/cda/files/ES05GATES.pdf (accessed online May 28, 2007).

Gates, B. http://www.illinoisloop.org/quotes.html#survey (accessed May 31, 2007).

Ginott, H. www.enthink.com/quotations/teachers_and_teaching/ (accessed January 10, 2007).

Giroux, H. A. 2003. Racial injustice and disposable youth in the age of zero tolerance. *Qualitative Studies in Education* 16(4): 553–565.

Glew, G., M. Fan, W. Katon, F. Rivara, and M. Kernic. 2005. Bullies, victims, and their feelings about school. *Archives of Pediatrics and Adolescent Medicine* 159(11): 1004–1085.

Green Schools Initiative. http://www.globalgreen.org/greenbuilding/GreenSchools.html (accessed May 31, 2007).

Gurian, M. 2001. *Boys and girls learn differently! A guide for teachers and parents.* San Francisco: Jossey-Bass.

Gunzelmann, B. 2004. Hidden dangers within our schools: What are these safety problems and how can we fix them? *Educational Horizons 83*(1): 66–76.

Gunzelmann, B. 2005. Toxic testing: It's time to reflect upon our current testing practices. *Educational Horizons 83*(3): 212–220.

Gunzelmann, B. 2009. New possibilities for a new era: Research-based education for equality and excellence. *Educational Horizons 88*(1): 21–27.

Gunzelmann, B., A. Bachelder, N. Bourgeois, A. Jackson, A. McMaster, A. Meenan, S. Rivard, L. Twombly, and T. von Loendersloot. 2008–2009. Global Education/ Global Voices Research Project. Unpublished research, Southern New Hampshire University.

Gunzelmann, B. and D. Connell. 2006. The new gender gap: Social, psychological, and educational perspectives. *Educational Horizons 84*(2): 94–101.

Hansen, J. M. and J. Childs. 1998. Creating a school where people like to be: Realizing a positive school climate. *Educational Leadership 56*(1): 14–17.

Hirsch, E. D. 1996. *The schools we need and why we don't have them.* New York: Doubleday.

Hirsch, E. D. 2006. *The knowledge deficit: Closing the shocking education gap for American children.* New York: Houghton Mifflin.

Hoffmann, B. 1962. *The tyranny of testing.* New York: Macmillian.

Holt, J. www.quoteland.com (accessed January 10, 2007).

HomeSchool.com. http://www.homeschool.com/resources?ConnectionAcademy/default.asp (accessed March 22, 2009).

Hoy, W. K., C. J. Tarter, and J. Bliss. 1990. Organizational climate, school health, and effectiveness: A comparative analysis. *Educational Administration Quarterly 26*(3):260–279.

Hoy, W. R., C. J. Tarter, and R. B. Kottkamp. 1991. *Open schools/healthy schools: Measuring organizational climate.* Newbury Park, CA: Sage.

Hoy, W. K. and A. E. Woolfolk. 1993. Teacher's sense of efficacy and the organizational health of schools. *The Elementary School Journal, 93*(4): 355–372.

Hoyle, J. R. and R. O. Slater. 2001. Searching for accountability for a loving school environment. *Phi Delta Kappa, 82*: 790–94.

iEARN: International Education and Resource Network. http://iearn.org/about/index.html (accessed May 15, 2009).

Indoor Air Pollution and Health Problems. http://www.indoorpollution.com (accessed February 3, 2007).

Internet Public Library: IPL. http://www.ipl.org/ (accessed May 18, 2009).

InternationalEd.org. Losing Our Edge: Are American Students Unprepared for the Global Economy? http://www.internationaled.org/PISA.html (accessed September 7, 2008).

Kennedy, J. F. www.quotegarden.com/teachers.html (accessed January 10, 2007).

Kids Health. 2005. Coping with cliques. http://www.kidshealth.org/teen/your mind/problems/cliques.html (accessed May 18, 2009).

Kindlon, D. and M. Thompson. 2000. *Raising Cain: Protecting the emotional life of boys.* New York: Ballantine.

Klein, C. and M. Poplin. 2008. Families home schooling in a virtual charter school system. *Marriage & Family Review* 43,3/4: 369–395.

Koch, K. 2000. Zero tolerance for school violence. *CQResearcher* 10: 185–208. http://library.cqpress.com/cqresearcher/cqresrre2000031000 (accessed May 30, 2007).

Kohn, A. 2000. *The case against standardized testing: Raising scores, ruining the schools.* Portsmouth, NH: Heinemann.

Kohn, A. 2004. Safety from the inside out: Rethinking traditional approaches. *Educational Horizons* 83(1): 83–41.

Kozol, J. 1991. *Savage inequalities.* New York: Crown Publishers.

LDOnline. http://www.ldonline.org/ldresources (accessed May 20, 2009).

Lehr, C. A., Chee Soon Tan and J. Ysseldyke. 2009. Alternative schools: A synthesis of state-level policy and research. *Remedial & Special Education* 30(1): 19–32.

MacNeil-Lehrer News Hour. November 18, 1999. *Zero tolerance.* Newshour Extra: A Newshour with Jim Lehrer special for students. http://www.pbs.org/newshour/extra/features/july-dec99/zerotolerance.html (accessed May 29, 2009).

Magnet Schools of America. http://www.magnet.edu/index.php (accessed May 15, 2009).

Manthey, J. The boys project. http://www.boysproject.net/html (accessed May 21, 2007).

Mayo Clinic. 2006. Childhood obesity. www.mayoclinic.com/health/childhood (accessed January 30, 2007).

Mayo Clinic. 2006. Classroom of the future. Mayo Foundation for Medical Education and Research. http://www.mayoclinic.org/levine-classroom-future/1 (accessed January 30, 2007).

McEvoy, A. and R. Welker. 2000. Antisocial behavior, academic failure, and school climate: A critical review. *Journal of Emotional and Behavioral Disorders* 8(3): 130.

Meier, D. 2002. *In schools we trust: Creating communities of learning in an era of testing and standardization.* Boston: Beacon Press.

Meier, D. 2004. For safety's sake. *Educational Horizons* 83(1): 55–60.

Merrow, J. 2004. Safety & excellence. *Educational Horizons* 83(1): 19–32.

Merrow, J. 2001. *Choosing excellence: "Good enough" schools are not good enough.* Lanham, MD: Scarecrow Press.

Mosca, F. J. and A. Hollister. 2004. External control and zero tolerance: Is fear of our youth driving these policies? Book Review. *Educational Horizons* 83(1): 2–5.

National Association of Independent Schools. http://www.nais.org/ (accessed May 20, 2009).

National Coalition of Alternative Community Schools. NCACS. http://www.ncacs.org/ncacs.htm (accessed May 15, 2009).

National Center for Education Statistics. 1998. *The condition of education.* Washington, DC: U.S. Department of Education.

National Clearinghouse for Educational Facilities. Resources List: Color Theory for Classrooms and Schools. NCEF. http://www.edfacilities.org/rl/color.cfm (accessed May 20, 2007).

National Clearinghouse for Educational Facilities. Resources List: Mold in Schools. NCEF. www.edfacilities.org (accessed May 20, 2007).

National Clearinghouse for Educational Facilities NCEF. Resources List: School Cleaning and Maintenance Practices. http://www.edfacilities.org/rl/cleaning.cfm (accessed January 30, 2007; http://www.edfacilities.org (accessed May 20, 2007).

National Center for Education Statistics: NCES. 1998. http://nces.ed.gov (accessed May 20, 2009).

National Commission on Excellence in Education. 1983. http://www.illinoisloop.org/quotes.html#educationtheory (accessed May 21, 2007).

National Independent Private School Association. http://www.nipsa.org/ (accessed-May 20, 2009)

National Institute of Environmental Health Services. 2006. Asthma and its environmental triggers. NIEHS. http://www.niehs.nih.gov/oc/factsheets/pdf/asthma.pdf (accessed May 30, 2007).

National Institute of Health. 2001. NHLBI Reports New Asthma Data for World Asthma Day 2001: Asthma Still a Problem But More Groups Fighting It. NIH. http://www.nih.gov/news/pr/may2001/nhlbi-03.htm (accessed May 20, 2007).

National Sleep Foundation. 2007. How much sleep is enough? http://www.sleepfoundation.org (accessed August 14, 2007).

Northeast Sustainable Energy Association. Building green schools resource list. NESEA. http://www.nesea.org/buildings/greenschoolresources.html (accessed January 30, 2007).

Noonan, J. 2004. School climate and the safe school: Seven contributing factors. *Educational Horizons 83*(1): 61–65.

Nordenberg, T. 1998. *Miracle drugs vs. superbugs: Preserving the use of antibiotics.* U.S. Food and Drug Administration. http://www.fda.gov/fdac/features/1998/698_bugs.html (accessed May 18, 2007).

Northeast Sustainable Energy Association. 2001. Building green schools resource list. http://www.nesea.org/buildings/greenschoolsresources.html (accessed January 30, 2007).

Newberger, E. H. 1999. *The men they will become: The nature and nurture of the male character.* Cambridge, MA: Perseus.

Peterson, R.L. and R. Skiba. 2001. Creating school climates that prevent school violence. *Clearinghouse 74*(3): 155–163.

Peterson's Private Schools and Boarding School Search. http://www.petersons.com/pschools/code/psector.asp?path=hs.fas.private&sponsor=1 (accessed My 20, 2009).

Pollack, W. 1998. *Real boys: Rescuing our sons from the myths of boyhood.* New York: Henry Holt and Co.

Popham, W. J. 1999. Why standardized tests don't measure educational quality. *Using Standards and Assessment 56*(6): 8–15.

Population Reference Bureau. 1999. *Reports on America*. PRB.1 (1). http://www.prb.org/Source/ReportonAmerica2000CensusChallenge.pdf (accessed May 31, 2007).

Princiotta, D. and Bielick, S. 2006. *Homeschooling in the United States: 2003*, (NCES 2006-042) U.S. Department of Education. National Center for Education Statistics, Washington, DC.

Private School Finder. http://privateschool.about.com/od/usschoolsbystatea/l/blmap.htm (accessed May 15, 2009).

Private School Review. http://www.privateschoolreview.com/ (accessed May 20, 2009).

Rose, L. C. 2004. No child left behind: The mathematics of guaranteed failure. *Educational Horizons* 82(2): 121–130.

Rudner, L.M. 1999. Scholastic achievement and demographic characteristics of home school students in 1998. Education Policy Analysis Archives 7, No. 8. http://epaa.asu.edu/epaa/v7n8/ (accessed March 28, 2009).

Russell, B. www.enthink.com/quotations/teachers_and_teaching/ (accessed January 10, 2007).

Saltman, K. J. and D. Gabbard. (ed.) 2003. *Education as enforcement: The militarization in our schools*. New York: Routledge Falmer.

Santilli, J. 2002. Health effects of mold exposure in schools. *Current Allergy and Asthma Reports* 2: 460–467.

Schneider, A. and C. Smith. 2000. Major brands of kids' crayons contain asbestos, tests show. *Seattle Post Intelligence*, May 23. http://seattlepi.nwsource.com/national/cray23.shtml (accessed May 31, 2007).

Schultz, D. P. and S. E. Schultz. 2001. *Theories of personality*. Belmont, CA: Wadsworth.

Seligman, M. 1995. *The optimistic child: A revolutionary program to safeguard children from depression & build lifelong resilience*. New York: Houghton Mifflin.

Seligman, M. 1998. *Learned optimism*. New York: Pocket Books.

Sizer, T. R. and N. F. Sizer. 1999. *The students are watching: Schools and the moral contract*. Boston: Beacon Press.

Springer, S. and G. Deutsch. 1998. *Left brain, right brain—Perspectives from cognitive neuroscience, 5th ed*. New York: W. H. Freeman and Co.

Sternberg, R. Personal communication.

The Child Advocate. http://www.childadvocate.net/stateresources.htm (accessed March 22, 2009).

The Independent Schools Directory. http://www.independentschools.com/ (accessed May 20, 2009).

The Parent Advocacy Group for Educational Rights. http://www.pagergroup.org (accessed March 29, 2009).

Tirozzi, G. N. and G. Uro. 1997. "Education reform in the United States: National policy in support of local efforts for school improvement." *American Psychologist* 52(3): 241–249.

Unknown author. http://www.quotegarden.com/teachers.html (accessed October 10, 2009).

Unschooling.org. http://www.unschooling.org/ (accessed May 20, 2009).
U.S. Department of Education NCLB and Other Elementary/Secondary Policy Documents. 2004. http://www.ed.gov/nclb/landing.jhtml (accessed May 6, 2007).
U.S. Department of Education. 2001. PL107-110. http://www.ed.gov/policy/elsec/leg/esea02/index.html (accessed May 7, 2007).
U.S. Department of Education. http://www.ed.gov/index.jhtml (accessed May 20, 2009).
U.S. Department of Education. http://nces.ed.gov/pubs2006/homeschool/ (accessed March 25, 2009).
U.S. Department of Education Institute for Education Sciences Search for Private Schools. http://nces.ed.gov/surveys/pss/privateschoolsearch/ (accessed May 20, 2009).
U.S. Department of Education Planning and Evaluation Service Archived Information. http://www.ed.gov/offices/OUS/PES/int_activities.html#assessments (accessed May 31, 2007).
U.S. Census Bureau American FactFinder. U.S. Census Bureau, 2006 Population Estimates, Census 2000, 1990 Census. Retrieved May 21, 2007 from http://factfinder.census.gov/servlet/SAFFPopulation?_submenuId=population_0&sse=on.
U.S. Charter Schools. http://www.uscharterschools.org/lpt/uscs_docs/311 (accessed March 22, 2009).
U.S. Environmental Protection Agency. 1989. Recognition and Management of Pesticide Poisonings. EPA 735-R-98-003.
U.S. Environmental Protection Agency. 1992. Healthy lawn, healthy environment. Office of Prevention, Pesticides and Toxic Substances. USEPA. http://www.fda.gov/fdac/features/1998/698_bugs.html (accessed May 20, 2007).
U.S. Environmental Protection Agency. 1994. Reducing Radon in the schools: A team approach. EPA 402-R-94-008. http://www.epa.gov/iaq/schools (accessed May 20, 2007).
U. S. Environmental Protection Agency. 2002. Protecting children from pesticides. USEPA. http://www.epa.gov/pesticides/factsheets/kidpesticide.htm (accessed May 20, 2007).
U.S. Environmental Protection Agency. 2007a. Asbestos in schools publications. USEPA. http://www.epa.gov/asbestos/pubs/schools.html (accessed May 20, 2007).
U.S. Environmental Protection Agency. 2007b. Brownfields cleanup and redevelopment. USEPA. http://www.epa.gov/swerosps/bf/ (accessed May 27, 2007).
U.S. Environmental Protection Agency. 2007c. Green indoor environments. USEPA. http://www.epa.gov/iaq/greenbuilding/index.html (accessed May 27, 2007).
U.S. Environmental Protection Agency. 2007d. High performance schools. USEPA. http://www.epa.gov/iaq/school design/highperformance.html (accessed May 27, 2007).
U.S. Environmental Protection Agency. 2007e. Mold Remediation in schools and commercial buildings. USEPA. http://www.epa.gov/iaq/molds/index. Also, http://www.epa.gov/mold/moldresouorces.html#Mold%20in%20Schools (accessed January 30, 2007).

U.S. Environmental Protection Agency. 2007f. Radon in schools (2nd ed.). USEPA. http://www.epa.gov/radon/pubs/schoolrn.html (accessed May 21, 2007).

U. S. General Accounting Office. 1994. Indoor Air quality. School facilities: America's schools report differing conditions. GAO Report #HEHS-96-103. http://www.gao.gov/ (accessed May 20, 2007).

U.S. Government's policy on class size reduction. http://www.ed.gov/rschstat/eval/other/class-size/index.html (accessed November 16, 2009).

U.S. Secret Service & U.S. Department of Education. 2002. The final report and findings of the safe school initiative: Implications for the prevention of school attacks in the United States. Washington, D.C.

Virtual Schooling Home Schooling. 2006. http://nces.ed.gov/pubs2006/homeschool/distancelearning.asp (accessed May 20, 2009).

Vogel, S. 1990. Gender differences in intelligence, language, visual-motor abilities, and academic achievement in students with learning disabilities: A review of the literature. *Journal of Learning Disabilities* 23(1): 44–52.

WebMD. 2000. Teen Sleep Deprivation A Serious Problem. WebMD. http://www.webmd.com/news/20000821/teen-sleep-deprivation-serious-problem (accessed August 14, 2007).

Welsh, W. 2000. The effects of school climate on school disorder. *Annals of American Academy of Political and Social Science* 567: 88–107.

Wenar, C. and P. Kerig. 2000. *Developmental psychopathology: From infancy through adolescence.* Boston: McGraw-Hill Higher Education.

Winfrey, O. Special report: American Schools in Crisis. http://www.illinoisloop.org/quotes.html#survey (accessed May 31, 2007).

Wolk, R. 2004. Thinking the unthinkable. *Educational Horizons* 82(4): 268–283.

World Health Organization. 1992. The Classification of Behavioral and Mental Disorders. ICD-10.

ZTNightmares.com. 2003. *Zero Tolerance Nightmare Stories.* http:// ztnightmares.com/html/other_stories.htm (accessed May 20, 2007).

About the Author

Betsy Gunzelmann is chair of psychology at Southern New Hampshire University and has been teaching at the college and graduate levels for approximately 20 years. She has also worked for a number of years in the schools as a counselor, psychologist, and consultant. She completed her undergraduate degree in elementary education and then went on to earn two master's degrees—one in elementary education and the other in guidance and counseling. She received her doctoral degree from Boston University.

www.ingramcontent.com/pod-product-compliance
Lightning Source LLC
Chambersburg PA
CBHW021852300426
44115CB00005B/128